"*Sincerity Uncompromised* is a s
to become a classic in the realm of Self-discov̶e̶r̶y̶...
easily connect with the mind and heart of any genuine seeker of ̶T̶r̶u̶t̶h̶.
He is a powerful authentic teacher—wise, subtle, deep, compassionate
and accessible. Seek him out."

—Mooji, spiritual teacher

"This beautiful book is a must read for everybody who wants to find
their inner jewel. Ameen's way of staying in touch with his own authentic core in the midst of life challenges and adversity is truly inspirational. His journey depicts a refreshing sincerity. Other than the depth
of his spiritual awakening, which blessed him with true freedom, he
also describes the remarkable process of awakening to his soul-nature
—a rarely described development that moved him into a life of greater
peace and wholeness. This book is unique in that it simply, yet powerfully, transmits the power of standing in your own truth."

—Patricia San Pedro, four-time Emmy award winner and author of
The Cancer Dancer—Healing: One Step at a Time

"This book is a valuable resource to practitioners who long to explore
deeper mystical realities but are committed to living their insights
amidst the challenges of daily life and relationship. Not stopping at a
more limited and transcendent notion of awakening, but allowing
himself to be taught and informed by the challenges that his early awakening brought—particularly in relationship to human intimacy, Ameen
inspires us to embrace both psychological and spiritual awakening
together as part and parcel of a sincere and fully lived human life."

—Mariana Caplan, PhD, MFT, author of *Eyes Wide Open: Cultivating Discernment on the Spiritual Path*

"Ameen's awakening was without the guidance of a spiritual teacher or lineage or the support of a tradition. He has crafted his own original path, focused only on the path of waking up and cleaning up. Not being in any tradition, his work is free from tradition and can serve as both an introduction and as an inspiration for the growing number of practitioners entering the Path, who are passionate about realizing their potential. The writing has a very personal, inspiring, and beautiful flow to it."

—Genpo Roshi, creator of the Big Mind Process, Abbot of Kanzeon Inc. and author of *Spitting out the Bones*

"What a welcome breath of fresh air! Ameen's *Sincerity Uncompromised* is the splendid voice of a spontaneously integral and integrative life-journey and teaching. Ameen's story and his wisdom speak directly not only, in his words, to our potential spiritual 'freedom from life', but also to our in many ways much more elusive 'wholeness in life.' This distinction, and the revelation of the 'seamless oneness' of these apparent opposites, have been the foundation of my own orientation and approach for over a quarter of a century. It's one that to this day, truth be told, I do not feel many teachers, never mind aspirants, have really grappled with in a no-holds-barred way.

The damn-the-torpedoes, unflinching experimental rigor of Ameen's lifelong inquiry into reality... his excruciating ordeal growing up as a highly sensitive boy and young man in the aggressive macho culture of Israel... the profundity of his eventual establishment in the consciousness that transcends all phenomena... his refusal to allow that freedom to become a shield against his vulnerability, his shadows, and the coming to life of his soul-nature, or an excuse not to embrace teaching, business, marriage, and parenthood—this book should be required reading for serious seekers of truth. More than that, it's a life-story and communication of whole-being common sense that anyone wanting a reliable compass for living in the 21st century would do well to take to heart."

—Saniel Bonder, Founder of Waking Down and author of *Healing the Spirit/Matter Split*

"I think Hans Plasqui has written a book that could and should become a classic of post-post-modern spirituality. It really gets us beyond the starting point—namely waking up.

What happens when you wake up in the morning? Do you say, oh great, I woke up, end of the journey? Not at all! It is just the beginning of a new day, just as birth and rebirth are the beginning of a new story, a new life, and a new cycle. That's why I found *Sincerity Uncompromised* so useful and inspiring because it explains in great, very interesting, biographical detail how waking up is a call to further development and creating our individual ego selves to be capable of dealing with and worthy of the gift of awakening. If this is not understood, we can very likely screw everything up and consider our little selves totally unique and thus super special, and start a cult or some other really annoying entity. What often happens is akin to mistaking the starting line of the race for the finish line, or, in other words, not realizing that the journey has just begun.

What this book emphasizes so beautifully is that the awakened journey must include a re-examination of, and redemption of, our individual personal self so as to become a vehicle worthy of the journey of enlightened nondual consciousness. I found *Sincerity Uncompromised* to be written with great intelligence, exactitude, honesty, and humility. It really is inspiring!"

—John Dupuy, founder of Integral Recovery and author of *A Revolutionary Approach to the Treatment of Alcoholism*

"*Sincerity Uncompromised* is an engaging account of Erez Levitin's path of awakening. This relevant and informative book looks at the practical implications of waking up in a modern world. Levitin's and Plasqui's distinction between spiritual freedom and psychological freedom is an important and insightful one. This book recognizes that spiritual development is more than just anchoring in the absolute, and advocates the value of whole-heartedly engaging life in the relative. Ameen's story highlights the continued, evolutionary wisdom of the soul's journey. Ameen's teachings seem practical and accessible. This book speaks to the value of shadow work and how it can enhance spiritual growth.

The biographical portion of the book is captured through a unique and engaging objective account of Ameen's journey, which is followed by an interview-style dialogue to capture his teachings. It's a clear, easy, enjoyable, and informative read."

—Cindy Lou Golin, PhD, Leadership Coach and Integral Facilitator Faculty; teaches courses on Shadow and Integral Theory and Practice

"The words 'spirituality', 'enlightenment', and 'awakening' have become hopelessly polluted with wrong-headed ideas, spiritual projections, guru-worship, and expectations that are so far removed from the real meaning and power of those words as to make them nearly useless. Ameen is offering a bold and brave take on how we might define a spiritual life and spiritual practice for the 21st century and beyond, one rooted in a grounded understanding of what awakening really is—and isn't. Deep spiritual insights can change your life in ways you can't imagine, but they are also no magic bullet. There is no escaping our humanness, our psychological shadows, our bad morning breath, or so many other things that make us such noble, and such flawed, creatures. Ameen demonstrates that awakening will take you to your knees, and is also the most ordinary and everyday thing you can ever experience. This book is must-read for anyone seriously on the path to awakening, where liberation isn't about transcending life but about awakening inside the pull and push of the everyday. Read this and gain a much better and more accurate understanding of what the journey of awakening is really all about."

—Keith Martin Smith, Zen priest and award-winning author of *A Heart Blown Open: The Life and Practice of Zen Master Jun Po Denis Kelly Roshi.*

SINCERITY UNCOMPROMISED

Ameen

NEW SARUM PRESS
UNITED KINGDOM

SINCERITY UNCOMPROMISED

First published by New Sarum Press May 2021

Copyright © 2021 Ameen (Erez Levitin) and Hans Plasqui

Copyright © 2021 New Sarum Press

Cover Photo: Stanislav Kutac

ISBN: 978-1-8383836-1-9

NEW SARUM PRESS
www.newsarumpress.com

This book is dedicated to you.
May you find peace and happiness in this lifetime.
Lots of love
Ameen

Table of Contents

INTRODUCTION

H AVE YOU EVER WONDERED... WHETHER IT IS possible to change so profoundly that you see yourself and the world through different eyes? Whether a life of freedom, clarity and a sense of wellbeing, that far surpasses your present condition, can be yours? Are you curious about what it means to wake up, in a radical way, to who you really are? If you are, then this book will surely strike a chord in you... It is an intimate sharing of the inner journey of awakening into freedom, by a contemporary spiritual teacher called Ameen.

If we examine our inner world up close, we will notice that we spend most of our time lost in thought. We talk to ourselves incessantly; telling ourselves the same stories over and over again; as if there were somebody else in there with us, who missed out on every single thing that has been going on with us—some fictitious character that needs to be updated non-stop. We keep mulling over yesterday's experiences, and worry about what tomorrow will have in store for us. Most of the time our thoughts are jumping around rather capriciously and randomly. We are diligently engaged in an endless inner monologue, producing a ceaseless stream of words and images. In the midst of all this mental chatter, we are often taken in tow by regurgitations of shadow reactivity and emotional patterns—and they too have a way of repeating themselves ad nauseam.

If we then probe a bit deeper into our interiors, and hone in on the undercurrent of all this mental-emotional restlessness, we might notice an undefined sense of subtle anxiety; a basic existential contraction we simply feel unable to release. This is the bedrock our sense of self stands on.

If we look over the workings of our interior apparatus as a whole, we notice that it operates largely involuntarily and unconsciously—and it does so around the clock. Whatever else can be said about our inner state, its typical quality is usually not one of open attentive presence, fully relaxed into whatever is arising right now—not one of freedom, clarity and a sense of wellbeing.

In the meantime, we have grown so used to this condition that its actual quality virtually passes us by unnoticed. Most of us go through life, convinced that the state of mind we live in every day is our natural state. We have come to presume that it is simply our plight—an inevitable situation, intrinsic to the human experience. But how legitimate is this presumption really?

Many of us have experienced brief glimpses of a different reality—fleeting moments in which the constant stream of thought, and the obtrusiveness of our emotional patterns, are brought to a sudden halt. Perhaps we have been struck by the exquisite beauty of a sunset; entered a flow state during sports; felt ourselves merge with the formidable harmonies of a Schubert string quintet; marveled at the miracle of childbirth; or perhaps, we were simply overcome by the transcendent majesty of infinite space and its countless sparkling stars, while gazing up into the night skies. In those fleeting moments, we accessed a different quality of our consciousness—a quality in which our ordinary sense of self and its endless stream of emotions, thoughts and images dropped away momentarily, making way for a more profound state of being.

In response, some of us may have wondered: What do such experiences tell us about the actual potentials of human consciousness? Could it be possible to live from a depth of being, prior to the thick layer of our everyday existential anxiety—not just briefly touching base with it, during fleeting moments of awe, wonder and flow, but truly living from such a depth, in an enduring way?

It is not a secret that sages, mystics and contemplatives throughout the ages have answered this question with an affirming yes. They have always insisted that if we simply pause for some time, and scrutinize our state of mind with precision and care, we too will come to find out that there is indeed such an alternative. It *is* possible, they maintain, to spend our lives in a much more favorable condition than the one that is presently ours. It *is* possible to relax our mental-emotional machinery to such a degree that the trance of our compulsive emotions is lifted, and the spell of thought is broken once and for all. And this, they say, is an extraordinary relief—as when the clouds part, after a heavy rainstorm, disclosing the radiant blue sky that was always already there anyway.

When such a breakthrough occurs, our sense of being a separate entity—anxious and afraid—dissolves away. What is left has often been described as impossible to capture in words, yet has nevertheless been communicated time and again with utterances like: radical freedom, vast spaciousness, luminous clarity, imperturbable silence, and a perpetual sense of wellbeing. Those who have woken up to this part of their nature maintain that *this* is our natural state; our true condition; the one we continue to overlook, even though it is always closer to us than our own heartbeat.

This book attempts to capture some of the particulars of the process of waking up to this more profound reality, as it occurred in Ameen's case. By its very nature, the spiritual process is a subjective and greatly personal matter. Reporting on it is a challenge, because its details are often incredibly subtle, all too human, and at times deeply intimate.

Yet this book withholds nothing. It is written with the intent of speaking candidly, and with nuance and vulnerability, about the delicate intricacies of spiritual awakening. Reading Ameen's story brings the process of waking up closer to home, and presents it as something you can relate to. Some of his struggles might very well be your own. But even if others are not, the candor and sincerity with which they are told will inspire, encourage and support you on your own journey.

The way this book came into being was more like one of those fortunate concurrences, rather than a carefully planned out project.

I first met Ameen at a New Age festival in Germany. If the ambition of this fair was to overwhelm its visitors with a wide range of competing New Age ideas and colorful paraphernalia—and instill in them a sense of spiritual indigestion—it was already successful by the time you had walked through the first aisle. Whether you were into alternative healing, the spookier interpretations of quantum physics, quick-fix self-help courses, psychic powers; or into the more serious forms of spiritual practice and human potential development—anything that smacks even remotely of esotericism or spirituality was represented in the countless little stalls, spread across the multi-floor congress hall.

After having wandered around a bit, curious but somewhat disoriented, I slipped into a room that felt more sober and quiet. I learned that a satsang—spiritual discourse—was about to take place there. Given everything I had taken in by now, my expectations weren't exactly high. As soon as everybody had settled in, a bold man in his early forties, athletically built and looking vibrant, entered the room and sat down in front of us. He radiated a silence of presence. We all sat there, waiting for satsang to start, but he remained quiet and simply kept gazing at us for long stretches of time—sometimes well past the point the average comfort zone would allow for. Yet his gaze was natural and unselfconscious, and had a quietening effect on my mind. After a while, I relaxed into the occasion, getting accustomed to the idea that this was going to be it for this session. Time passed. He spoke a few phrases now and then, left long gaps of silence in between, and continued to gaze upon us some more. Then it was over, and I wandered back into the hustle and bustle of this colorful festival.

As I was making my way through the crowded halls once more, it became apparent to me that something about my experience was different. An intriguing shift had taken place in my awareness—as if my sense of self had expanded to encompass the whole building. Rather than feeling as if I was wandering through the festival halls, I now felt as if somehow the whole event was occurring *within me*. With that, my feeling of being hopelessly submerged in this multitude of impressions was gone. *I* was no longer submerged *in them*; rather, *they* were submerged *in me*. There was a spaciousness, a lightness, a transparency, a serenity, and above all... a deep sense of silence.

This experience, which sitting in Ameen's company seemed to have helped facilitate, aroused my curiosity about him. He was not a quick-witted entertainer of crowds, or a clever word magician, of which there were several in this place. His impact seemed to be of a different kind. He radiated a palpable silence—a serenity that was infectious. Sitting with him seemed to have the power to draw you into your own depth.

Several months passed before we met again. This time, he invited us for lunch after satsang, and I had the chance to talk with him more personally. While munching on our pizzas, I inquired about his life and inner state. His demeanor was easygoing and he had a naturalness about him. It didn't take long before we dropped into a profound consideration about the nature of awakening. He was remarkably open for a first conversation and spoke with candor about the many struggles he had had to go through in his journey of waking up.

What was intriguing was that, rather than emphasizing his awakening into consciousness, he mainly talked about the many post-awakening challenges he had to face, before he felt that his realization of consciousness had truly settled in, in a deep, solid way, and had blossomed into a certain maturity. His willingness to speak openly about this delicate terrain was exciting. This first interview, which we now jokingly refer to as our "pizza-interview", marked the beginning of a truly creative collaboration.

After the pizza-interview, both of us felt we had only scratched the surface of a rich, profound and multidimensional subject—something too interesting not to be deepened and teased apart further. So we decided to lock ourselves up for a week in a quiet room in Berlin, Germany—where Ameen lived at the time—and explore all the details of his inner journey. From morning till sunset we talked about all the challenges, questions, doubts, confusions, insights, breakthroughs and setbacks involved in Ameen's process of awakening. During that first week, so much was brought to the surface that we both agreed to continue our exploration, take it further, and perhaps... even write a book about it.

After several more of these wonderful weeks of joint seclusion and in-depth dialogue in Berlin, we got together in Ibiza, Spain a couple of times, and later continued our exploration in Tel-Aviv, Israel, where he often spends the winters. The transcriptions of our dialogues served as the source material of this book—and I began to work with this material, to distill Ameen's spiritual biography from it; and transform it into a structured body of teachings.

As such, this book is set up in two parts. Part one—the spiritual biography—tracks the unfolding patterns of Ameen's process of awakening, as well as many particulars of his further maturation process *after* awakening. Part two—written in dialogue format—presents Ameen's core teachings. It instructs us in the many ways we can support and nourish our own transformational process of both waking up into spiritual freedom, and growing up into further human maturity.

Because of Ameen's keenness to share his understandings about life *after* awakening, the book as a whole is permeated with a post-awakening flavor. As such, it takes us beyond the classical account of someone's spiritual awakening. It boldly ventures into the heart of rarely described territory: the nuts and bolts of the post-awakening world.

If we look at Ameen's journey from a bird's-eye view, there are a several ingredients in it that make his an intriguing case—perhaps even an anomaly.

What jumps out at you immediately is that he has never been a classic spiritual seeker. In fact, he never even showed much interest in spirituality. He only wanted to be free. He didn't draw on the guidance or support of a spiritual teacher, nor did he lean upon the nurturing context of a spiritual tradition. He is a stand-alone figure, who traversed the path of waking up in his own self-crafted, original way, using only his sincerity as his inner compass. This is unusual. The lack of a supportive spiritual context, more often than not, complicates the spiritual process. In Ameen's case, however, a different dynamic was at work—a force powerful enough to bend these less than ideal conditions: his relentless passion to be free, no matter what.

From his early youth in Israel, he wanted nothing more than to grow intimately close to life—a closeness so complete that it would be free from any dissociations. He wanted to be capable of living life to its fullest. To him, such a non-separate intimacy with life was what genuine freedom would taste like.

Yet the stark contrast with his actual reality couldn't be more dramatic. Whatever he tried, a fierce sense of isolation remained present underneath it all—as if there was a gap between himself and life... and he *had* to close it. For a long time, all his attempts to do so seemed futile. The environment in which he grew up didn't support his aspirations much either. In fact, the notoriously loaded cultural atmosphere of Israeli-Jewish society intensified his sense of isolation even further. During his teens he began to grasp how the dissociative tendencies in his cultural conditioning kept triggering the separative patterns of his own mind—and it began to dawn on him that he had to liberate himself from both of these impediments.

Because Ameen's early struggle was mainly about facing up to his shadows, and hence psychological in nature, he initially understood freedom to mean *psychological freedom.* He had no idea that freedom, when pursued to its fullest, could be so profound that it could result in a radical shift in consciousness—a state of *spiritual freedom*, far surpassing the domain of psychology.

At the age of thirty-two he woke up as this spiritual freedom. He recognized himself to be consciousness itself; one with everything. As a result, his lifelong sense of isolation dissolved in a deeply significant way.

Much to his surprise, though, he soon found out that his inner journey was far from over. In spite of the obvious profundity of his awakening, it began to dawn on him that this transition only marked the beginning of a further process—a process he came to refer to as the 'post-awakening developments'. He realized that, even though he had *recognized* his non-separate nature, he hadn't yet *become* it in such a way that it had saturated every part of his being. He noticed that, at times, the clarity of his awareness would momentarily be compromised by old shadow material resurfacing, and in those moments there was still—however briefly—a separation from life. He understood that so long as these shadows had not been dissolved, he wouldn't be able to fully live his awakened nature all the time.

This insight set in motion a further maturation process which Ameen calls the 'crystallization of the mind'. During this process the mind is purified from residual shadows, reactivity and negative conditionings that might still be lingering in the caverns of the psyche after awakening. As this purification process forges ahead, the mind becomes more and more transparent—and the light of consciousness begins to shine through it more brightly.

At some point, explains Ameen, the entire body-mind begins to take on a quality of translucence. This is the time when a deeply subtle part of us, that we have always intuited, but have never really fully been aware of, begins to disclose itself. It is sometimes referred to as our soul-nature, and it can be felt as a subtle energy dynamic, gently persuading you to express that delicate personal flavor that is yours and yours alone. It is your innermost unique essence—that which inspires you to bring out your latent potentials, and thereby draws you into a further completion of your life course. As such, the emergence of the soul-nature further enriches the quality of awakening.

In line with his original inclination—to grow intimately close to life—

Ameen describes the gist of these post-awakening developments as a process of integrating the formless nature of consciousness with the fullness of life. In his case, this movement back down into life was marked by extremes.

Right after awakening, he felt as if he couldn't be further removed from life. He was so deeply absorbed in his own interior, relishing the radiant beauty of consciousness, that life no longer exerted even the slightest pull on him. He only wanted to merge into all that splendor—and die into his own bliss. It took the awakening of his soul-nature—and with that, the recognition of a personal destiny *in* life—to reverse that movement again, and reorient him back towards life. A 'return to the market place' as the famous Zen proverb would have it.

As consciousness and life became more and more integrated, Ameen's awakening took on a more mature quality. It had now moved well past the point of the mere recognition that his true identity was consciousness itself, free from any of its contents. It had thoroughly sank in; saturated the depths of his being; and blossomed into the extraordinary freedom he had always been drawn to from the very beginning—a non-separate intimacy with life.

What is striking in Ameen's case is that shadow work has played such a major role in his journey. This is somewhat unusual. In today's spiritual culture, shadow work is often seen as an additional practice; as something you do upon occasion, when some unyielding obstacle threatens to hinder the smooth flow of your life. There is good reason for this auxiliary status. Shadow work does not, in and of itself, have the capacity to catalyze growth into higher consciousness. Reaching down into the unconscious, and re-integrating repressed energies into the self, is not the actual mechanism by which waking up occurs. Waking up requires the mechanism of self-transcendence.

Still, shadow work can greatly contribute to creating a situation that is conducive for awakening. In some cases it is even a necessary prerequisite, especially when a significant amount of energy, attention and awareness is bound up in self-contraction, and only a limited amount is left for further growth. Under such circumstances the spiritual process may lack the necessary momentum to catalyze a breakthrough into self-transcendence. It risks stagnation. In such cases, shadow work becomes vitally important. It liberates this locked up energy and revitalizes the body-mind, which, in turn, makes a breakthrough into self-transcendence more likely.

To some extent, it is precisely this effect of shadow work that seems to have played a significant role in Ameen's awakening. Shadow work prepared the ground for the self-transcending impulse to come alive in him—an impulse to which he was already intensely oriented, as the silence he felt to be his deepest core.

So his growth trajectory tells the story of a dynamic struggle between deepening the silence of awareness and the noisy pull of neuroses, snatching him out of that silence again and again—until at last, all the turmoil comes to rest in the crisp clarity of a deep and imperturbable silence, which he recognizes to be his true self.

One of the key insights in Ameen's account is that the depth of one's awareness—that capacity for open attentive presence with whatever is arising—and the density of one's shadow constellation impact one another reciprocally and profoundly. As such, this book explores in detail how shadow issues can impede the process of awakening, and how, even after waking up, they can still continue to sabotage the true promise of an awakened life.

For Ameen, an awakened life is utterly free, and at the same time deeply human and profoundly sane. In the final analysis it means both spiritual freedom and human maturity. "Spiritual freedom"—Ameen says—"is the realization that your true identity is consciousness itself, rather than just the body, the mind or the soul. Human maturity is your capacity to manifest your true identity as consciousness *with* your body, mind and soul. It is the art of translating oneness into daily life, and manifesting truly enlightened virtues—like goodness, truth and beauty—as much as is humanly possible." For him, this is the bottom line of awakened living. Clearly, this is forever a work in progress. Showing up this way requires moment to moment integrity. It calls for a continuous commitment to scrutinizing oneself with the freshness of beginner's mind—even after awakening. And such a stance, so much is clear, can only be upheld when it is rooted in unwavering sincerity... a sincerity that is uncompromised.

So at its most intimate core, this is first and foremost a book about the power of sincerity. By sharing how this mysterious quality has shaped his life, Ameen hopes it will be enlivened in you too, take you in tow, and orient you towards your own true north.

For where does sincerity truly come from... if not from that part of you that is already awake? What is it really... if not the voice of your inner-most nondual heart—calling you back to itself?

Hans Plasqui
Ghent—Belgium, 2019

When the Sirens Wailed

> *A person who is beginning to sense the suffering of life is, at the same time, beginning to awaken to deeper realities, truer realities. For suffering smashes to pieces the complacency of our normal fictions about reality, and forces us to become alive in a special sense—to see carefully, to feel deeply, to touch ourselves and our worlds in ways we have heretofore avoided.*
>
> KEN WILBER, *The Simple Feeling of Being*, p.73.

A WAILING SOUND FILLS THE AIR ALL OVER THE city. Its sharp noise cuts right through my bones. I shiver. I am supposed to stand straight, take on a dignified pose, but I shrink as the commanding sound overtakes me. I just stand there, a fragile Israeli boy, fearfully frozen, as the sound builds momentum. Growing louder and louder, it sends waves of collective mourning and national pride across my country.

It is Holocaust Remembrance Day—Yom HaShoah—the day on which Israel commemorates the six million Jews brutally murdered in the Holocaust. Every year again on 27 Nisan at 10:00 am sharp, sirens wail all throughout the country for two minutes non-stop. During this moment people suspend all activities and stand to attention. Life in our vibrant cities comes to a halt. Traffic stops. Even on the highways, drivers get out of their cars and stand still in the middle of the road. Was there ever a hustle and bustle on the sidewalks? In these moments it's as if it might never have been. Vendors in the once swarming street markets stop shouting, transactions in our shopping streets cease, teachers stop teaching, classes go quiet. The entire country comes to a standstill as people pay silent tribute to those who lost their lives under Hitler's Nazi regime.

Every year again, the sirens' warning would communicate a clear unspoken message: six million of our fellow countrymen had died, so that we could live on this special plot of land. We were all raised with the sense that we were indebted to our country and our people; that we were the lucky ones who were given the opportunity to live here because of the terrible price our ancestors paid. The call of the remembrance sirens was society's way of confirming our ethnic identity and emphasizing what binds us together as a people.

I can still remember the sense of intrusion that came over me during this yearly ceremony. It felt like an invasive attempt to mold me into something I was not; to inject a false identity into me—a story of Jewish mourning that I, as a young boy, had very little to do with. From an early age I experienced society as having no regard for who I really was. This kindled rage and scorn in me; feelings that were always hidden behind my boyish smile. I felt repressed by our cultural message, as if the core of my very being—that uniquely personal essence that desperately wants to emerge out of every child—was being stifled; as if the real me was being choked, while a collective self-image was being groomed to take its place. It felt like a piercing infraction of my integrity, and it created a constant nagging pain in me; a pressing sense of confinement, as if I were locked up in a corset of steel.

To my young ears, the sound of the siren at Yom HaShoah somehow came to epitomize all these feelings. It stirred up an inner cry that had slept deep within me, and along with that, an intense yearning to break free. From early on, a firm resolve was running through my veins: *I am going to be myself, no matter what.*

But right now, despite my resolve, and with the sirens' reminder in my ears, I am obliged to stand still with my fellow classmates and show loyalty to our collective suffering. Finally, after the two minutes that always seem like an eternity, the sirens stop, and class resumes. I sit down on my chair in silence and, like a hedgehog, curl back into my own intimacy—the space of refuge that I know as the real *me*; a space of inner quietude that has been familiar to me from as early as I can remember.

Going within and hiding in my cocoon always helped me cope with the pain, and it was there that I got an early taste of true silence. Little did I know back then that my emotional suffering would reap such a fruit in the years to come, and that the intimate space of refuge I knew to be my authentic self would deepen so profoundly that it would become my inner strength.

Yet on that day, once again—when the sirens wailed—I withdrew, hiding deep within to avoid a pain that never seemed to cease, and robbed me of all hope of ever finding release.

1

Isolation: My Core Dilemma

I longed for a life that reflected the tender space of silence that I felt to be my deepest core; a life in which I could be sincere without fearing to be crushed for it; a life in which love and respect were pivotal values. No longer did I want to sacrifice my own authentic self to the glory of a collective self-image that did not resonate at all with the deepest features of my personality.

ON OCTOBER 23, 1966, I WAS BORN AS EREZ Levitin, in Ramat Gan near Tel Aviv. My mother told me that as a baby I often preferred to sleep rather than eat. As far back as I can remember I always carried an uneasy background sense of not fully fitting in this reality. As a toddler, I would stand on the edge of the playground, and silently watch the other kids play. In social situations and noisy places, I immediately felt confined, as if my freedom were being impinged upon in these jittery and disruptive places. Yet, in contrast to that, as soon as I turned within I felt comfortable. As long as I can remember, a sense of intimate quietude has been constant in my life—a space of intimate stillness where I felt truly at home.

As I grew toward adulthood, my personality formed itself around this natural essence of quietude, and I developed character traits such as sensitivity, tenderness and introversion. As is always the case, the many forces that shape the contours of our personalities are subtle. They are often unconscious, and hard to spot. Primal influences like family, parents and society are often the most powerful ones, and under their influence some of my innate qualities blossomed. Others were stifled and converted into shadows. Consequently as I grew older I developed feelings of shyness, inferiority, insecurity, shame and guilt—shadow qualities that seemed to come along easily with my quiet nature.

Our family lived an upper middle-class life in a modest villa in Herzelia—a small town near the coast of Israel, just a few kilometers north of Tel-Aviv. It was one of the wealthiest neighborhoods of Israel, with a cosmopolitan flavor, as many diplomats lived there. My father owned a computer company, and my mother was a teacher. Materially, my brother, my sister and I had everything we could ever hope for. The atmosphere in our family was free and casual; there was often music playing in our house; our doors were always open; and a stream of friends was constantly coming and going. My parents were very liberal and valued freedom. They never asked me to think or behave a certain way, and gave me plenty of opportunities to explore life, and pursue my own freedom.

As is the case with many of us, one of the most influential forces to leave an imprint on my personality was my relationship with my mother. She is a Holocaust survivor, and her life has been marked by the atrocities of war. There is little doubt that some of the residual trauma of her heartbreaking life history trickled down into the way she related to us. As a little girl during World War II she was hidden in a chicken coop in a Polish farmer's barn. For two and a half years, she lived with the chickens, suffering from malnutrition, and coping with the harshest living conditions imaginable. The farmer was paid by my grandfather every month to make sure he wouldn't give my mother away to the Germans. When the war was over, and my mother was finally picked up by my grandfather, she was still wearing the same dress as when she arrived. She could hardly walk, and the doctors gave her little chance of surviving; even so, the love and care of my grandmother eventually managed to pull her through.

My mother's life story left a residue of sadness within that was always tangible underneath her gentle, loving demeanor. There were periods during which she locked herself up in her room and cried for days on end, because she felt as if everybody was hurting her. Yet despite her tragic moods, she would always carry on and push forward. The unspoken message I received from this was that life was a painful, difficult ordeal, and that people were cruel. Yet my mother's perseverance taught me to face life and always keep going, despite adversity and hardships.

At times I got the feeling that I had to make up for the fact that my father was often absent. As I was the eldest son, my mother often shared her troubles and heartaches with me. In such moments I became her emotional support which was a heavy burden to such a young and sensitive boy. Our bond was so deep that I used to feel her pain as if it were my own. I often felt guilty for her grief, for her pain, as if I were somehow responsible. It made me want to stay close to her and support her. The prospect of leaving her alone with her sorrows was all too often at odds with my own natural drive as a young lad to set out into the world and pursue my autonomous way through life.

My mother had other idiosyncrasies that impacted me profoundly, especially her unspoken attitude towards men. I often got the sense that she considered masculinity to be primitive and negative. She seemed to feel that traditional masculine traits like being sexual, outgoing, strong and firm went against women's integrity. The message I picked up from her attitude was that being alive to your own masculinity was somehow a violation of the feminine—and for a long time I lived with the belief that to pursue my own masculinity was inferior, coarse and rude, and somehow equated to hurting women.

My mother's ambivalence towards masculinity was matched by her love of feminine qualities. She was deeply compassionate, full of heart, and her whole way of relating to me gently oriented me towards greater sensitivity and kindness. Even so, like any parent, she was not without her expectations about the sort of person I should be. I can still remember the seemingly innocent way she would talk about me to others: "Erez will always behave well... He is a decent kid." For all their kind intentions, there was an undercurrent, and I often felt profoundly disempowered by such utterances. I heard them as glorifications of my weaknesses, turning my shyness, shame and fear into some desirable condition to be maintained at all costs.

My father's powerful personality, too, was not supportive in developing my own inner strength. He came across as serene, centered, and always on top of the game. To him, being able to keep calm, while radiating strength and showing kindness to others, was the measure of freedom. But this was a façade and the force of repressed aggression and dominance was always tangibly present—and was sometimes unleashed. When he believed people had crossed his boundaries, or were inconsiderate towards him, he did not hesitate to get into fights.

I can still remember how we drove off in our car one day for a family trip. A big army truck abruptly cut us off the road. My father was furious, floored the throttle, passed the truck and stopped it. He commanded the soldiers to get out and demanded to know who was the driver. When the perplexed soldier identified himself, my father slapped him in the face, and we drove off. I remember many such incidents.

At times Father was physically violent towards us. I can still recall how he was joking with friends that he had intentionally lowered the head rests in our car so that he could slap us without having to stop the car. I feared those hands of his. There was something quick and violent about them.

As I entered my teens, Father's blunt and forceful interventions became increasingly embarrassing to me. One time he turned up— from nowhere—at the gym where I was working out. He picked up some weights and started to lift them. He simply wanted to show off to me and my peers that he could do it just as well as I could. Another time, when I brought my girlfriend over to our house, he showed up half-naked, wearing nothing but a sarong, so that he could show off his muscular chest to her. It is not hard to imagine the mortification I felt about his macho displays.

In many ways, his manner of relating to me interfered with my psychological growth into a confident, independent man. Whenever he was around I felt as if my youthful aliveness was being suppressed. He always had ways to make sure I wouldn't—or felt that I couldn't—stand up for myself. In his presence, I was pushed back into my own weaknesses, fears and insecurities. The fact that such a powerful character unconsciously served as my role model made me feel even more insufficient. His influence magnified my already deep fear of society—the fear that it might violate my integrity, just the way my father did. My mother, in all her kindheartedness, couldn't help me here. Her parental power collapsed in front of his forceful presence. She could only watch how everything went according to my father's wishes.

Yet in spite of the fact that I felt emotionally repressed by him, some of the values for which my father stood played a key role in the formation of my personality. He taught me to question authority; he continually encouraged me always to stay true to myself no matter what; and he definitely fueled my drive for freedom.

So while both my parents contributed in many valuable ways to the development of my character, they also intensified a sense of repression in me. Both in their own unique way added to the tempering of my life energy. As time progressed, I came to feel as if an entire storehouse of vital energy was being curbed within me, and this perpetual energetic contraction made me lose touch with my inner strength.

This was the psychological atmosphere in which I entered my early teens—the time in which Jewish boys become Bar Mitzvahs, 'sons of the commandment', responsible under Jewish Law. Bar Mitzvah, which occurs at age thirteen, traditionally marks the transition from boyhood into manhood. But when my time for this auspicious occasion had come, I didn't feel like a man at all. I looked skinny and pale. My posture was hunched over, which was an outward reflection of my inner insecurity and shame. Not only did I look skinny and frail, I was also often unwell. I was subject to powerful allergies that often resulted in respiratory illnesses.

5

My mother, in accordance with her compassionate nature, wanted me to become physically stronger and healthier, and asked my grandfather to buy me a surfboard for my Bar Mitzvah. How I loved this gift! At first, I was so weak that I could hardly carry the board to the beach, but soon surfing the ocean waves began to strengthen my body and open up my sickly lungs to absorb the fresh sea air. Paddling all alone in the vastness of the ocean and floating quietly on the water, while I watched for the right moment to catch the next wave rolling in, instantly connected me back to myself. The silence I experienced while surfing was always a refreshing break from my perpetual sense of repression. To me at the time this was freedom. Soon I revived physically, and my allergies disappeared. Yet for all the relief this offered me, no amount of surfing seemed to be able to dissolve my sense of repression with any sort of finality. On the contrary. As time went on, my inner conflict had grown more intense—as if this friction had become part of my persona somehow; a persistent psychological pattern that I couldn't break out of.

As I grew further into my teens, this pattern of repression continued to weigh on me. I began to become aware of how my emotional condition was also nourished by another source—one in which I had been immersed all my life, but that I hadn't been cognizant of, until now: the Jewish-Israeli identity.

A particular ethos reverberates through our culture; an underlying sentiment that shapes our collective self-image. It is a sense of frustration, fueled by the fear of being under threat all the time—an incessant anxiety, infused with a feeling of being special; of standing apart from the rest of the world. By the time I became aware of this collective sentiment, it had already impacted me profoundly.

Living in Israel felt like living in a pressure cooker. I could sense a restlessness and a nervousness everywhere. Emotional mechanisms like aggression and defensiveness were easily triggered, and lurked in all corners of daily life. They colored the basic human interactions: people pushing themselves to the front of waiting lines; inconsiderate drivers in traffic; rude words on the sidewalks... People acted with a habitual defensiveness. Anxiety was part of everyday existence, and this underlying emotional atmosphere was nourished and kept alive by the harsh political realities in which we all grew up.

When I was seven years old the Yom Kippur War broke out. I remember how we had to cover the windows with black paper to prevent enemies from spotting the light, and how my mother and I had to flee into cellars to be safe from enemy fire. When I was twelve, I witnessed a terror attack while walking home from school. A group of Arab terrorists had hijacked a bus and were engaged in a fire fight with the police, not so far from my home. The mere sight of it was deeply disturbing to my young mind. It made the scary stories we heard all around us come alive—stories about how terrorists would enter our cities by boat, break into our houses, and kill anybody they could find. For some time after seeing that attack on the bus I had trouble sleeping. I lay awake at night, afraid that terrorists—or even Nazis—would break into my bedroom and kill me in my sleep. Incidents like these were part of being Israeli; it was what we knew and it was our life.

As children, we were all raised with stories of how the Jewish people carry a colossal historical weight on their shoulders. Ever since the Roman army destroyed the temple in Jerusalem in 70 CE, our people have lived in exile. During this long history, they suffered massacres, persecutions and expulsions by Church and Mosque, as well as casual, cultural persecution. As a result, a strong sense of victimhood pulsates through our culture, and this is exactly the message Israeli society projects all around: we have been victimized for as long as we can remember; our land is constantly under threat from outside enemies, and we need to defend ourselves.

It is a logic feverishly promoted by authority figures and politicians representing our society, and it is often presented as a grand narrative, loaded with historical and religious references. So, while growing up, we often heard emphatic messages along these lines:

7

"Israel is the land of our forefathers. The land to which Abraham brought the idea of One God, where David set out to confront Goliath, and where Isaiah saw a vision of eternal peace. We are God's Chosen People. The 4,000-year-old historical bond between the Jewish people and the Jewish land is undeniable. Israel will always reserve the right to defend itself. We will protect our borders and ourselves against Arab terrorism, and all other outside threats. Too many Israelis have lost loved ones. When we say *never again*, we *mean* never again. Our nation finally arose from the ashes of the Holocaust. The right of the Jewish State to exist should never again be denied."

This is the general thrust of our dramatic storyline as a people, and it is ever-present in our collective mindset, right up to the present day.

This ethnic identity can be read as the result of a historical journey of our collective psyche from victimhood to aggression—an aggression fueled by the need for self-protection. The message reverberating through society is that there is no other place for us to live but here, in the land of our forefathers, and that the country will offer us protection against the hostilities of the outside world. Participating in this national logic means becoming a protector yourself. So, from very early on, we were all groomed to become protectors of the nation.

Perhaps nowhere do we find the Israeli ethos more distinctly expressed than in the yearly sequence of our national and religious holidays, and days of remembrance. The more I became familiar with the meanings of all these occasions, the more I became uncomfortable with them. As I grew up, it was no longer just the wailing sirens at Yom HaShoah that made me feel confined. I felt the same around all such occasions that celebrate the Jewish-Israeli identity. I saw their annually recurring sequence as an attempt to instill in us the sense of collective identity that made me feel so suppressed. Our land has its rhythm, and that rhythm keeps its story alive. Whatever the actual events commemorated by these holidays, to me the basic message always sounded the same: how we—a small group of people—managed to prevail while the world conspired against us, and how our unusual history was indicative of our special status as the Chosen People. The very thing from which many of my fellow countrymen derived their sense of belonging, seemed so terribly empty to me. For most of them, these holidays were a celebration of our uniqueness. For me, their meaning enforced in us the sense of psychological separation from the rest of the world—and they nourished my own feeling of separation from life. So rather than seeing our holidays as honorable opportunities to pay tribute to our past, I saw them as mere cogs in a pre-programmed conditioning machine; incessantly repeating the same old chatter; glorifying our collective narrative, until it would leave a lasting emotional mark on us, that would then be passed on to the next generation.

All throughout my teens I felt as if our collective self-image kept me in a stranglehold. I could sense the contraction—the lovelessness—in our extreme focus on ethnic identity. It was all around us, and it made life narrow and uptight. It was there in the way in which army generals were being adored as role models; it was present in the ways in which the media presented anti-Semitic incidents abroad; it was at the source of our perpetual dehumanization of the Arab population; it was hidden in the subliminal messages of many of our advertisements, in which even female models were often expected to express a touch of masculine strength. Our culture is governed by an ethos of conflict, victimization and self-protection, and these sentiments translate into values like toughness, strength and aggression, which, over time, have become the deep features of our collective identity.

So, to fit into this society and participate in it, a young person has either to build up a thick mask of toughness, or simply be endowed with a strong natural presence. If not, it's hard to gain respect and avoid being stepped on by others. More often than not, gentle qualities like tolerance, sensitivity and forgiveness are perceived as weaknesses. Rudeness, aggression, power and hot-tempered defensiveness are valued as signs of character strength and, since all of these qualities were diametrically opposed to my own, they would trigger shyness and fear in me. The intrusive nature of the Israeli mindset pressed all my buttons. I simply did not know how to cope with it. My innate sensitivity didn't allow for the aggressive lifestyle required to function smoothly in society. To many people in my environment, my personality traits were a sure sign of feebleness. They clearly had a different ideal of what an Israeli male should be like, even though I was still just a kid. In this society, bent on raising future soldiers, even we children were expected to demonstrate the strength and toughness of a grown-up. Unsurprisingly, I felt deeply frustrated about the message I was getting from my social environment: that who I was, was insufficient and not acceptable. All throughout my teens, this frustration built...

I remember how I hated school and experienced my teachers as cold, hard and unloving. Most of them were of East European descent and brought with them a belief that children must be educated harshly. I can still recall how, one day, my teacher asked me to come up to the blackboard. I stood there, my usual self: somewhat shy, insecure and slightly hunched over. The teacher couldn't stand such an embarrassing sight and made fun of me in front of the whole class: "Stand like a man! Why don't you stand like a man?" Even though, from the outside, the incident probably didn't look that dramatic, inside I felt humiliated—crushed! It left a deep scar in my psyche. In that moment it felt as if the very essence of my entire existence was declared to be wrong and inadequate, in front of all my classmates. My most intimate nature was not being valued, and the one thing that I cherished most—my inner quietude—was being ridiculed.

Something in me broke, and I remember it as the day I gave up on society and external authority definitively.

From that day onward, I knew deep down that going along with the cultural ideal was simply not an option. An inauthentic compromise like that would only keep me feeling confined, and increase my emotional anguish. I knew I had to take care of myself, and grow strong in my aloneness. There was no other way to free myself from my own neuroses, and from this collective self-image that kept triggering them all the time. I longed for a life that reflected the tender space of silence that I felt to be my deepest core; a life in which I could be sincere without fearing to be crushed for it; a life in which love and respect were pivotal values. No longer did I want to sacrifice my own authentic self to the glory of a collective self-image that did not resonate at all with the deepest features of my personality. Those insignificant few moments at the blackboard marked a turning point in my life.

I didn't have a clue how I would have to discover what I was looking for, but I simply felt ready to give up on the status quo and take a leap into the unknown. With that readiness came a rebelliousness against society and authority. I began to fervently reject our cultural conditioning and pursue my own integrity—a move for which I knew no reward was going to come my way.

Time passed, and I watched my life turn into a battle between pressures to conform and the urge to be myself at any price—an agonizing condition from which only my surfboard offered me some temporary relief. So, all throughout my teens, I continued to love surfing, even though it wasn't a popular sport at that time in Israel. It was more of a California thing, but exactly because it was so atypical, it never failed to give me a refreshing break from Israeli culture. Surfing had a cosmopolitan aura and was embedded in a lifestyle that valued freedom and individuality—values that I loved. It gave me the chance to connect with like-minded people. Through surfing I found a place in society that resonated with my authenticity. Its curved motions spoke of elegance and softness and felt like cutting right through the Israeli spirit of toughness. I loved this movement and the release it offered me so much that when there weren't any waves, I made sure I surfed the paved roads with my skateboard instead, just to experience the same sense of elegance, lightness and spaciousness. But even so, I still knew full well that it wasn't my genuine answer. It did not have the power to uproot the contraction at the core of my uneasy predicament. So, any breathers were always short lived.

By the time my friends started to date girls, the reality of my condition hit me once more, and this time, it did so with a vengeance. Even though I was a good-looking young man, I lacked that extra edge in my efforts to approach the other sex. I just couldn't find that assertive outgoing energy within myself. Whenever I tried to connect to a girl, words wouldn't come out. It was sheer agony. So, girls didn't show much interest in me, and even if they did, their interest would wear off quickly, because I wouldn't respond to their signals. I was too passive and quiet. I just didn't know how to get out of my own shell. I felt cut off from my inner masculine power, and I couldn't figure out what was going on with me. Whatever I tried, I just couldn't break the spell of my own psychological patterning. So I simply suffered the consequences.

The subsequent years were spent in turmoil. My shyness intensified further and the little self-confidence that I had left disappeared. I was living behind a virtual wall. On the other side of it was life, freedom, girls. I felt as if I were slowly suffocating. Inside my anger built. I had to break free.

I decided to change schools. Maybe, it would be easier to start afresh, make new friends and date girls, if I could leave my reputation behind. My new school had a vibrant social life, and there were plenty of pretty girls around. But it didn't change a thing. I came to see that simply changing external circumstances wouldn't help. Something more radical was required. With the dawning of that understanding, my interest in studying faded away. I decided to drop out of high school, seven months before graduation. I wanted to dedicate all my time to solving my problem. I needed to work on my self-confidence and find my masculine strength. So instead of spending my days in a school room, I decided to go to the gym and immerse myself in training to weightlift. The day after leaving school I was already down on my back in the sports hall, trying to lift the lightest bar. I felt weak but determined. In the back of my mind, I was convinced that by developing my body I would end those agonising times of feeling weak and would finally get the recognition from the opposite sex that I so longed for.

Since I was no longer in school, I had plenty of time to dedicate to my physical practice. The rewards came quickly. Within six months I had changed my physical appearance completely. But more importantly, I began to see that the choice for change was in my own hands, and that with dedication and determination I could shape my own reality. I stopped looking for the approval of others so much and became more comfortable just being *me*—an autonomous *me*. When I looked in the mirror I now saw a more masculine image, and when I looked within I felt more connected to my male energy.

Yet despite this visible change, underneath it all, I knew I still hadn't really landed in my own power. I still hadn't truly embodied what I had hoped for: a spontaneous self-confident skill at interacting fearlessly with other people; nor had I acquired that extra edge to approach the other sex freely. My psychological condition had improved slightly, but it hadn't yet become the in-depth transformation that I longed for. Despite my muscular body, I still couldn't connect to the core of my own strength. Frustration grew, as life was still largely out there, unreachable, on the other side of my virtual wall.

Soon my emotional life became even more complex and paradoxical. On the one hand, I felt strong and proud as I stood firm in my aloneness. On the other, I longed for true connection with others. But the truth was that I didn't have a clue how to open up to those others. I feared that the moment I expressed myself with authenticity, I would be rejected. Deep inside I could still sense that authentic space of tenderness, intimacy and quietude that had always been my core. But it felt so delicate and vulnerable that it was utterly out of sync with the prevailing values and expectations of almost everybody in my immediate environment. So unsurprisingly, I was afraid that if I were truly to be myself, my integrity would be compromised, and I would lose myself in the process.

These emotional dynamics had made me shut down, in an attempt to protect myself against the presumed intrusiveness of the outside world—and that reaction had entangled me in a pressing emotional dilemma: An intense yearning to embrace life was burning in my heart. I wanted to grow intimately close to it. Nothing felt more important to

13

me. But instead, I felt deeply isolated. I continually felt a gap between myself in here and life out there, and I wanted to close it. Yet however much I tried, I couldn't figure out how to break the spell of this sense of separateness.

Amidst all the emotional turmoil, only one thing stood out crystal clear to me: I *had* to break free from this sense of isolation, and I was willing to do anything it would take to tear down my prison wall.

My resolve was not based on a well-considered choice. It was deeply instinctive. The whole set of superimposed expectations and ideals about how a person was supposed to be, felt like a tight skin enveloping my body, and I simply wanted to rip it off. I felt as if I were being strangled. There was a desperate urgency to it all. My desire to break free dominated my attention day and night.

While other kids were busy figuring out whether they wanted to become a doctor, a pilot or a lawyer, or how they could best plan their futures in order to function successfully in society, I pictured myself as a free man; deeply involved in life; without fear or shame; liberated from the repression of expectations and the burden of our collective past. At the same time, I would be innocently immersed in the love, the wonder and the mystery of life. And even though it all seemed so far off at the time, I could sense it was a real potential. I felt that goodness, truth and beauty were out there, and that life was too precious to be compromised on by lesser ideals.

During a time when everything was in doubt, this intuition was my secret way to cope with my nagging sense of isolation—an emotional predicament that would shape the twists and turns of my life path, all the way up to liberation.

2

The Army: Stronghold of the Israeli Identity

My psychological ordeal had connected me to a tremendous source of inner strength. It was the strength of the human spirit that always takes over when we are left with no other choice than to go forward against all odds; it was the power that is liberated when we step out of the victim role and take full responsibility for our situation.

WHEN I TURNED EIGHTEEN MY TIME HAD come to join the Israeli army. For many Israelis, serving in the army to safeguard homeland security is a consolidation of their national identity. They consider it as an opportunity to put into action everything they know themselves to be as citizens of their country. To many, the sense of military duty has the force of a blood oath. It is an unquestioned moral obligation. Not joining the army is on a par with social suicide. As such, the army is a cornerstone of our collective self-image, and perhaps, one of its most telling icons.

I was called up to the army in 1984. At that time, Israel was still deeply involved in the Lebanon War. Many Israelis, and many more Lebanese, Syrian and Palestinian combatants, had already lost their lives in the conflict. I can still remember the daily media reports about all the soldiers that had been killed. Nothing about the whole idea of enrolling in the army and partaking in this madness was appealing to me. I simply didn't want to go, and as far as I was concerned, it was non-negotiable. My refusal wasn't out of fear of becoming another media statistic in the Lebanon War. I just did not want to partake in any endeavor that nourished, maintained or even celebrated the values our collective self-image was built on. To me the army symbolized the very mindset I had struggled with and against all my life. Joining up would be on a par with jumping into the system's jaws, and saying farewell to my integrity. I had put my mind on breaking free from my cultural conditioning, and I was determined to pursue that intention.

But like all my peers, I was called in by the army to get pre-tested and assess which type of army unit I would be best suited to serve. I passed all my medical tests with flying colors. My psychological examination, however, revealed a different reality. It exposed my real feelings towards the army. Unsurprisingly, my less than appreciative attitude didn't go down well, and I was sent straight to the office of the army psychiatrist. During a brief session I expressed my aversion to the values I believed the Israeli society was built on, and my utter lack of desire to protect them with my life. My psychiatric profile was aptly diagnosed as 'low motivation to serve'. I felt happy with this assessment. It gave me hope that my troubles would soon be behind me, now that my truth was out in the open.

But the army officers were unimpressed. They had their own solution for cases like mine. They enrolled me in a special program for society's outcasts, designed to train a wide variety of people, from criminals and drug addicts, to kids from broken families and individuals with various psychological disorders. We would all have to go through an adapted form of army training, aimed at turning us into soldiers after all; and we would also receive a supplementary education to make us fit into society again.

The program turned out to be tough. It was filled with formulae of harsh discipline, and we were treated with condescension and disrespect. In between, we had to listen to commanders bragging about their heroic feats in Lebanon, in the hope that these role models would inspire us somehow. I felt trapped in hell. Not only did I actually end up in the army, I was also in a program with the crudest and most problematic segment of society. Not surprisingly, I couldn't connect with anybody, let alone create friendships. Complete alienation set in.

By the start of the second week, something snapped inside. I panicked and ran off into the sand dunes. I didn't stop until I reached the nearest highway. There I hitchhiked home. By the time I had arrived there, I realized that there would be dire consequences for this act of disobedience. I had done something unthinkable. But I didn't care. I knew that if I wanted to remain true to myself, I had to push it even further, rather than simply accept my punishment, and comply with the rules of their game. I figured that I had to do something so extreme that it would make the army authorities grasp the severity of my despair and leave me alone.

I decided to stage a fake suicide attempt. I believed that if they realized that I was so desperate that I wanted to kill myself, I would definitely be discharged.

My parents weren't home that day. So I opened my father's closet and took out his hunting rifle. I wanted to pretend that I had tried to shoot myself but missed or regretted it at the last second. I sat down on the couch in my bedroom and fired a shot. The bullet went right through the door, hit the ceiling of the hall, and landed on the floor, not far from where my sister was sitting. Severely shocked, she ran out to the house next door and came back with our neighbor. Not sure what was going on, he positioned himself in a safe place behind the door, reached his arm into my room and asked me to hand over the rifle to him. I simply obeyed and collapsed on the bed in emotional exhaustion.

The next day our army commander came to our house to make up a file about the incident. The whole event didn't have the result I had hoped for. The army simply brushed it aside, and within two days I was sent back to my base. In those days it was virtually impossible to get discharged. The army occupied a powerful place in Israeli society. It exuded an allure of untouchability and it was hard to deviate from its ways.

The subsequent weeks of my training were an ordeal. I slid into a depression. My commanders didn't know what to do with me, so they just left me alone. They no longer pushed me to partake in the special training program. Instead, I was assigned a job as the personal driver of an army colonel. It was an easy duty close to where we lived, and so I would go back home every afternoon, as if I had a regular job. But as the weeks passed by, my inner state worsened. I was sucked into the downward spiral of my depression and felt powerless to stop myself from sliding downhill.

I realized that I had to try once more to get myself out of this insane situation. I needed to make a forceful gesture that was impossible to ignore and state my case in an irrefutable way. I decided to stage another suicide attempt. I believed that if it looked more serious than the previous one, it would be bound to create the intended effect. This time I told my plan to my parents because I needed their help. I wanted to swallow an overdose of pills and be taken to the hospital. They were outraged by the idea, and told me in no uncertain terms that they would not participate in such madness. They didn't believe that I was actually going to go through with it. But I was determined and unstoppable at that point.

So, one evening, after coming home from the army, I went to the closet in the bathroom, took out all the pills I could gather, and swallowed them. Most of them were different medications my parents used. Within twenty minutes, I started to feel very nauseous. My body temperature began to fluctuate, going from overheated to ice cold, and back again. When my mother found me, she couldn't believe what I had just done. I implored her to take me to the hospital. At first, she refused, not suspecting the seriousness of the situation. But as my temperature kept fluctuating wildly, she realized the severity of my physical condition. In a panic she drove me to a first aid clinic, where I was put into an ambulance and driven to a bigger hospital. Even though my body felt terribly nauseous and my mind felt stressed, I remember lying in the ambulance, experiencing a background sense of deep peace. I felt I had done the right thing, trying to save myself from being programmed into the Israeli story by one of its staunchest representatives. After my stomach had been pumped out I stayed in the hospital for one more day.

Then the army took over again and transferred me to their psychiatric hospital for observation.

As I was regaining my strength, the army psychiatrists interrogated me, trying to grasp why I was behaving in this dramatic way. Whenever they questioned me, I was baffled by their total lack of care and understanding. They were not really interested in my motives. They were still trying to figure out the best trajectory for me to continue my military service. They were not trying to help me. Their agenda was simply to figure out how I could be used best as an asset for the army. Their attitude strengthened my resolve to continue enacting my self-assigned role as the guy who wanted to kill himself because he couldn't endure his predicament as an Israeli soldier. And so I did.

My family became ashamed of me and stopped visiting. My father couldn't cope with such rejection, as it had always been his dream to give me his own military badge so I could proudly wear it on my uniform. As liberal as he seemed, when it came to his Israeli identity, he was deeply patriotic. But even for my mother, who had never wanted me to serve in the army, the whole ordeal was simply too much. Yet despite my family's lack of support, I was relentless in my resolve to get out.

After about a month of daily meetings with the army psychiatrists, they finally came to the conclusion that it was probably better to discharge me. In a last effort to convince me otherwise, I was brought into a room, facing ten psychiatrists sitting in a half circle around me. All of them tried to get through to me about the serious consequences of my 'low motivation to serve'. They explained in no uncertain terms how I was going to be shunned by Israeli society; how a jobless future was awaiting me out there; and how I would be looked upon as an outcast for the rest of my life. They asked me again and again, with increasing emphasis in their voices: "Are you sure you want to go through with this?" In a final attempt to accommodate my lost cause, they offered me an easy gardening job for only once a week. But I simply wanted out. When they finally realized that all their efforts had been fruitless, they discharged me from my military duties. A heavy burden fell from my shoulders. I was free at last, and it felt so good. I had been in the army for exactly four months.

For a brief time, I was enthralled by a sense of relief and lightness. I valued the simplest things like talking, eating or sleeping as life's most precious gifts. Soon, however, the reality of my condition hit me hard again. Four months of intense emotional struggle, without the support of anyone, had taken a high toll. I started to feel as if my passion to live was seeping through the cracks of my broken personality. I began to doubt the wisdom of my decision to decline my military duties, and I started to become seriously concerned—even scared—about its possible consequences.

Everything they warned me about on that final day in the army came true. My social life deteriorated further. I felt so ashamed that I didn't even try to get a job, and people began to look at me disapprovingly. I had always presumed that, if only I could stay true to myself, I wouldn't care about what others might think of me—but suddenly I did care. Everybody else my age was wearing an army uniform, and I didn't have a clue how I could possibly legitimize to them why I wasn't. I felt powerless in the face of their invasive inquiries. I lost my trust in life and in myself, and I developed an even greater anger towards the army, society and authority. I felt as if all my options were blocked. I couldn't even enroll for any further studies anymore, because I had never finished high school. In the back of my mind, a vague vision of going out into the world and discovering my truth began to emerge, but I didn't feel strong enough to be undeterred and pursue it. In fact, I felt more alienated than ever. The virtual wall between myself in here and life out there seemed unbreakable.

I descended into a severe depression and started to suffer anxiety attacks. Most of the time I stayed at home and did nothing. I used to sit up on my bed in the middle of the night, wondering whether other young people also suffered the way I did; and I had a hard time getting up in the morning. I deeply longed for a social life, great friends, good fun and the hugs of a girlfriend, but I felt powerless to make it all happen. At times I would cry uncontrollably for no reason, as if my depression opened up all the psychological wounds I had accumulated in my life. Even my hair started to fall out as a result of stress. At the age of eighteen looks are important and the last thing anyone wants is to age prematurely. But nature took its course, irrespective of what I wanted. I was slowly going bald and along with my hair went my self-esteem. It was all too much. I got stuck in my depression and didn't have a clue how to muster the strength to break out of it. All my attempts to do so felt like climbing a marble wall.

My parents no longer knew what to do with me and decided to have me admitted to a psychiatric hospital. The psychiatrist to whom I was assigned came across as cold and clinical, and even from my distorted perspective I could tell that he saw me more as a case than as a person. He prescribed me pills that made me feel dazed and assessed me as being incompetent to cope with life, because I didn't fit in the army system. I quickly understood that his treatment wasn't going anywhere. It was based on the very same perspective that I wanted to get out of. Continuing with this approach would be the same as giving up on my truth and allowing our societal conditioning to take over once more. The only bright spot during my stay in this hospital was that I began to become clearer about the nature of my depression. I began to understand it as an unconscious act of self-pity—a form of waiting for my salvation—and I realized that I could only lift myself out of it by assuming full responsibility for my condition. This insight was like waking up from the numbness of a dream, and it helped me touch base again with my inner strength. Meanwhile, my treatment program simply continued. Nobody in the psychiatric hospital noticed my change of attitude. But after a while, my mother began to pick up on my inner shift—and began to doubt the effectiveness of my treatment. After some consideration we decided that it was time to leave the medical approach behind, and look for a different alternative—one that would be more adapted to my needs.

We found another psychiatrist. His approach contained more personal warmth, care and understanding, and I could sense that his attitude was more likely to be fruitful for me. During our sessions he simply allowed me to be myself, and his genuine attention created an atmosphere in which my self-confidence slowly started to recover again. He was just present with me, listening with empathy. He did not appear to judge me according to any preconceived model. I remember telling him that I felt as if my real identity was crushed; that my personality had vanished somehow; and that it needed to be rebuilt from scratch. He confirmed that I needed to go through a healing process and advised me to relax and stop worrying about my situation. I tried to follow his advice. But even with this softer approach, my recovery still proved to be a tough fight between my will to live and the lingering forces of depression. At times, it felt like I was pulling one foot out of a swamp, while the other was being sucked back in even deeper. I realized that in order to overcome my demons, I needed to create structure in my life. So I dedicated myself to a disciplined lifestyle and pursued it with diligence, even though at times it felt impossible. I started working out again. But even though I loved this particular discipline, it still wasn't easy to muster.

I remember how I would take the bus to the gym, and how halfway through the ride, out of the blue, a gust of sadness would overtake me. I would begin to ask myself why I was doing this and I would promptly get off the bus and take the next one back home. The next day the same thing would happen again, right in the middle of my workout, and I would give up and go home. There were many defeats like that. But I kept pushing myself until I managed to keep a consistent routine, supported by the memory of how, after a workout, I felt physically reborn and psychologically satisfied. Nevertheless, my overall psychological condition was still very weak and my nervous system was so fragile that it couldn't stand even the slightest pressure—especially from authority.

My inner predicament became glaringly obvious on several occasions. I remember how I found myself a job as a waiter. Yet on the very first day, when the boss asked me to do something, I just broke down in tears, left my tray on the table and ran out the door in panic.

There were many such incidents, and it was obvious that I still had a long way to go.

After about three years of struggle, with the help of my psychiatrist, and a lot of determination, I had finally managed to rebuild a healthy self. I had regained a decent degree of integrity and self-confidence and had succeeded in slowly lifting myself out of my depression. Slowly but surely, my life quality began to take on a new flavor...

I picked up high school again, where I left off, took my final exams and received good grades. With that, my opportunities for further study opened up again, and my hopes for a brighter future were rekindled. I got a job as a courier and made some money. At the end of every working day I felt joyful and free because I had got through the day without falling into sadness or panic. I was out in the world and felt fine about it. I had not only regained my sanity but had also matured.

My psychological ordeal had connected me to a tremendous source of inner strength. It was the strength of the human spirit that always takes over when we are left with no other choice than to go forward against all odds; it was the power that is liberated when we step out of the victim role and take full responsibility for our situation.

As my psychological turmoil had subsided I had slowly regained connection with that familiar place of inner silence, which had been my anchor since early childhood. More than before, I could now feel that this was who I really was. Reconnecting with this inner place revived my aspiration to stay authentic, and maintain my integrity at any price, rather than mold myself into somebody else's ideal. It was liberating. I felt as if the entire sky had opened up in front of me. All I needed to do to was say 'Yes!' to my deepest yearnings and fly out.

I knew the time had come to leave Israel. I was twenty-two and wanted to get a fresh start in a new place. I wanted to pursue my adventurous spirit and explore the world. Meanwhile, I had also developed a passion for photography and wanted to study it. So, I took a leap into the unknown and applied to a university in Toronto. I was accepted and moved to Canada to pursue a degree in visual communications.

My first year of studying felt like resting after a storm. I cherished the sanity of being away from Israel. Every day after classes I spent the rest of the afternoon just being in my room by myself, listening to New Age music on the radio. I enjoyed my aloneness so much that I wasn't interested in the regular student life of socializing and parties. The joy of being alone was nourishing and sufficient. The culture in Canada was a refreshing relief to me. It didn't push my buttons the way the Israeli style did. It was easygoing, respectful of personal space, caring, considerate, sensitive, accommodating and gentle—almost diametrically opposed to the atmosphere I felt in Israel. The Canadian style was a better match with my own nature. Interestingly enough, the stark contrast exposed my own typically Israeli traits, which I heretofore had only noticed in others. Against the background of the sensitive Canadian mannerisms, *I* was sometimes perceived as inconsiderate, not respectful, overly critical, all too judgmental and demonstrating an attitude of suspicion towards others. I realized that many of the traits that I disliked in the Israeli mindset were also in me. In many ways I *was* the society I criticized.

In retrospect, this was the time when it began to dawn on me that I needed to stop blaming society for my own neurosis. I wasn't just a helpless victim. I was the co-creator of my own predicament. The delicate interplay between cultural conditioning and personal neurosis exposed itself to my mind's eye. It became obvious to me that to close the unacceptable gap I experienced between myself and life, I had to work through both the cultural residue that was still within me, and my personal neurosis. This understanding set in motion a lengthy process of dis-identifying from my ethnic imprint, and it marked the beginning of my search for psychological freedom.

Towards the end of my time at university I started to feel restless again. Even though I had friends— even a girlfriend— and did what I loved to do, it wasn't sufficient. Something was missing. My yearning to relate to life in a deeper way grew stronger, and a nagging sense that I hadn't lived life to the fullest began percolating into my awareness. I felt that my youth was ending, and wanted to fully experience whatever was left of it. I remember writing in my diary that I felt like taking a leap into the unknown. I wanted to celebrate life; embrace it with open arms; get down and dirty with it; get some experiential scars; and live through whatever it would have to offer me.

My university years had given me a decent platform of sanity, but nothing more than that. My life conditions had become more favorable. But I could see that it would take a lot more than enhanced life conditions alone to solve my primal frustration of feeling separated from life. I had to go deeper, and address the problem at its root. It was time to move on to something new. I felt I was not ready to disappear into the system, find a job, start a family and go along with the status quo. So, I pondered my options. Should I look for a permanent job in Canada? The chances of success were rather slim, since unemployment rates were high at that time. Should I go back to Israel then? I knew I had arrived at a decisive turning point in my life, and so I thought about my future for a while.

With increasing clarity I saw that what I wanted most from life was freedom—and I figured that a great way to be free, and live life to the fullest, was traveling. To me, living an unstructured life of being on the move all the time, immersing myself in all kinds of situations, somehow reflected the spontaneous nature of life itself. So, I figured that traveling spontaneously, without too much of a plan, would surely help me get closer to the very pulse of life. I reasoned that if I could put myself into many different situations, I would have to learn how to respond to all of them appropriately, and as a result become more outgoing and connected.

I worked as a photographer at a ski resort at the time. Yet even though I had a job, I had little money. One of my colleagues told me I could earn good money in Japan teaching English. I decided to give it a try. My intention was to make some money and then travel around in Asia. I would photograph the locals, experience life's adventures, and learn about myself. After that I would come back, find a good university in the USA and take a Master's degree in communication. I wanted to work in radio and TV, create interactive programs and connect to people that way. A great program was being offered in Boston at Emerson College, and I wanted to apply for that. But first I would explore the world. I felt confident that my decision to take a leap into the unknown was the way to move forward.

And so, an intense five-year period of traveling began...

3

Reveling in Being

...my childhood suffering gave me an advantage over most others. It made it easier for me to take the leap into a careless, carefree approach that proved to be evolutionarily efficient, rather than simply immature and irresponsible. My entire journey throughout Asia was steeped in this wonderful spirit of freedom and surrender—a spirit that seemed to catalyze life's surprising generosity...

JAPAN WAS TERRIFIC, EVEN THOUGH LIFE THERE was tough. As a foreigner you quickly find out that it is a rather closed society. I couldn't find that job as an English teacher, and I soon ran out of money. I had sixty dollars left and my concerned family pleaded with me to come back home. But my resolve was firm. I was determined to prove to myself that I was capable of being on my own, enjoying my freedom and being self-sufficient. As I had secretly hoped, my limited financial means forced me to take initiative and become more outgoing. I decided to open a market stall in a train station in the middle of Tokyo and sell wooden handicrafts that I would import from Indonesia. The Japanese loved these trinkets and used them to decorate their office desks. I often used to work in the evenings after office hours, since my customers were hard-working family men coming back from work by train. I was very fond of the Japanese people and remember the beautiful connection I had with many of them. At times I was moved to tears because of the simple beauty of our interactions, even though I didn't understand a word they said. The market stall was a success. Its turnover was sufficient to live on. Taking matters into my own hands this way was an unfamiliar exercise for me. I grew up a spoiled brat who was provided with everything, and as a student, I had always received financial support from my family. I never really had to come out of my shell, take a stand and earn my living. Being provided for this way had definitely contributed to keeping me locked up within myself. But now the money started rolling in. For the first time in my life I was financially self-sufficient. I started to feel more connected to life and to my masculine power—the energy to go after what I wanted in life, and the firm resolve to get it. It was a real breakthrough.

When temperatures started to drop in Japan I traveled on to Thailand and Vietnam. I wanted to take a vacation and do some photography. Landing in Thailand was nothing short of a sensation. The country's luscious beauty made my attention shift to a different realm. Up until now it had been heavily focused on solving my psychological problems, acquiring a healthy functioning self and inhabiting my masculinity. But there, in the colorful delight of Thailand, an early sense of my spiritual nature started to unfold. I smelled the coconut trees and the ocean and forgot about everything.

I rented a small room for almost nothing in a guest house in the middle of the vibrant city of Bangkok. Everything felt perfect. I took long strolls through the lively city streets; enjoyed the exotic flavors of the cheap but tasty Thai food; and spent a lot of time simply lying on my bed, staring at the fan. I reveled in being alone and felt deeply fulfilled and free. I couldn't ask for more than just this. I felt completely self-sufficient—intoxicated with my own presence. I had no worries and no sense of future. I carelessly lived in the moment. I had no return ticket out of Thailand and had no idea when I was going to move on, or even what I would do the next minute. I enjoyed tremendously simply existing, nothing more. The fan in the room gave me air, the shower downstairs in the garden cooled my body. The colorful food and nightly walks in the hidden alleys of Bangkok filled me with excitement and wonder about life. I was immersed in the pleasure of the moment and couldn't possibly wish for anything else. I was out alone in the middle of Asia immersed in an intimacy with life that seemed to have no cause nor goal.

The quality of standing alone and feeling self-sufficient, that I had managed to get further in touch with in Japan, began to grow richer— but now it did so in a new way. This time it was not so much the result of action and asserting myself. It was brought about because I was sinking further into my own being and finding a solid centeredness there. A new sense of self-integrity emerged. I felt connected to my strength and completely fulfilled with my own presence. I relished the simple feeling of being. For the first time in my life everything felt just right. The utter beauty of it all had choked my mind and had dropped me into a state of rest, deep within myself.

The condition I was in left little room for questions or worries because my fear for the future had largely vanished. Occasionally fears and doubts about my current life course did come up again, and I documented them all in the endless pages of my diary. But even these occasional hard questions about my future plans, career, money and the realistic sustainability of my current lifestyle no longer had the power to stop me in my tracks.

As the months unfolded, I became more and more immersed in the deliciousness of being, and my concerns about my future simply paled into insignificance. While many of the youngsters around me felt that they had used up their free time and were considering going back home to get a grip on their lives again—find a job, start a family, or continue their studies—I couldn't care less. In Thailand the energy of my own presence came alive, and in all that splendor my whole plan of going back to university and taking my Master's degree in communication, simply vanished.

Starting from these carefree days in Bangkok, I allowed life to carry me forward as if on automatic pilot. To be able to get by, and finance my chosen lifestyle, I went back to Japan for a few months to make more money. Over time, I managed to create a sustainable balance between maintaining myself financially and following my nose. I wanted to explore this lifestyle of traveling without any plans to the fullest and find out how it could enrich me as a human being. So, I made some practical arrangements to prepare myself for the life of a long-term traveler. I assembled all my clothes, put them in a box, and sent them home. I only kept my backpack, two pairs of shorts and some other basic items.

And so, I kept backpacking throughout Asia, carrying only minimal necessities and my spirit of being young and free. I explored Vietnam, Indonesia, Thailand, Japan, India and also visited Australia. It was an intense and adventurous time, and I lived deeply in the present. During those years in Asia, a quality of simply being present gradually emerged in me and became the main flavor of my being. From Thailand onwards, my entire journey throughout Asia turned into one long meditation.

When I look back at this wonderful time in Asia, I can see now that a significant turning point in my evolutionary unfolding occurred during these years. It was an early spiritual awakening to my subtle nature, which I came to call *being*. Being is a spiritual state in which the ego is still intact, but it is no longer running the person exclusively. When we move into being, many habitual patterns of the ego and the mind begin to loosen up, and a deeper layer of the self starts to shine through. In Asia, I experienced a first expansion of my egoic self into that greater, more embracing and more intimate reality—and it allowed me to see that life carries a much deeper potential than merely acquiring a well-functioning ego. This expansion of my sense of self, and my deepening into being, would be the essence of my inner evolutionary unfolding for the next five years of traveling around. As the years went by, this beautiful, yet still somewhat immature spiritual state would blossom into further maturity... But at the time, I didn't have a clue that a still greater freedom was even a real possibility.

In many ways I had my painful past of growing up in Israeli society to thank for my irresponsible courage in letting it all go. I noticed that most of the other travelers I happened to meet, held tightly on to their concerns about building a career, making money and becoming successful. But I was able to give it all up quite easily. The severity of my childhood experience had convinced me that there was nothing more precious than following the sincerity of my own heart. So, I didn't experience the usual feelings people often go through when diverging from societal expectations: the guilt, the sense of inadequacy for not meeting the bar, or even flat out feeling like a loser. I could clearly see that all these emotional patterns had nothing to do with the reality of life itself. They were simply caused by societal expectations. They were the product of a collective ethos that we had all unconsciously interiorized during our early developmental process, and had then come to accept as the norm to live up to—a reference for the truth of life. So, my childhood suffering gave me an advantage over most others. It made it easier for me to take the leap into a careless, carefree approach that proved to be evolutionarily efficient, rather than simply immature and irresponsible. My entire journey throughout Asia was steeped in this wonderful spirit of freedom and surrender—a spirit that seemed to catalyze life's surprising generosity...

One day, while dining in a restaurant in Vietnam I met a beautiful German woman named Aloka. We started talking. It soon became obvious that we had many shared interests. We were both traveling around Asia, discovering ourselves and enjoying the spirit of freedom and adventure. We connected well, and a mutual attraction sparked between us. Yet despite that, our adventurous hearts inspired us to continue our own ways after a couple of days, and we lost touch.

Three months later, our paths crossed again in Thailand. Aloka had just returned from Poona, India, where she had spent some time in the colorful ashram-community of the infamous guru Osho—formerly known as Bhagwan Shree Rajneesh. She was obviously happy and had a certain glow about her: a gentleness, a silence. It was attractive. She started telling me about life in the ashram. But even though I was intrigued by her radiance, her stories about gurus, communities and devotees struck a cynical chord in me. I explained to her that I hadn't chosen this arduous way out of my cultural conditioning, simply to end up with some new version of it. What I really wanted was freedom from all forms of conditioning. I basically had no interest in eastern traditions, philosophies about enlightenment, or even spiritual freedom for that matter. For me freedom was psychological. It meant going beyond neurosis, personal blocks and shadow obstacles through psychological work. This was all I knew, and all I trusted as real, because that's what had proven itself to me through the changes in my life. But Aloka was clearly inspired and kept telling me about her experiences in Osho's ashram with great zeal. I loved her enthusiasm, but all the spiritual ideas she shared with me sounded overly complicated. I had always been moved by the sheer simplicity of life and did not entertain too many philosophical ideals about it. To me, the notion of enlightenment was nothing but a colorful exotic concept, reserved for old Indian males with long grey beards. I considered most stories about Indian spirituality to be cultural fantasies and had a hard time relating to them.

Back then, I didn't see any connection between the beautiful state of silence I was in and the spiritual concepts that were diligently being explained to me. I didn't know that, to a significant degree, I was already abiding in a place beyond the mind. I simply lacked the conceptual tools to understand where I was at, so I was very judgmental of everything I heard.

Aloka noticed my hesitation and decided to try to get through to me another way. She handed me one of Osho's books: *The Way of the White Cloud.* Her enthusiasm had roused enough curiosity in me and I started reading. As I kept turning the pages, I grew more and more surprised. Here was somebody who articulated my own understandings about life, society and freedom far better than I ever could. Osho wrote what I thought. This book confirmed my life's attitude and put into words the state of silent being I was experiencing. Still, it wasn't the great eye-opening *aha* experience for me. It was just nice to know that I was not alone with my ideas and that there was someone else out there with a similar outlook on life. The fact that this person happened to be a spiritual teacher gave me some trust that the way I was going about my life was okay, and that I was somehow still on track.

This time Aloka and I did not go our separate ways and our time together blossomed into a laboratory for evolution. In my mind my relationship with her was much more fruitful than any spiritual system could be. Both of us were deeply committed to our spiritual and psychological development. Right from the start we were always intensely communicative about our feelings, longings, drives, fears... in short, about anything that was transpiring in our interiors. We carefully watched and analyzed ourselves; scrutinized our habits and thought patterns; and gave each other unvarnished feedback. For hours, we sat together on the beaches of Goa, considering our projections on each other. We took long train rides deep into India, talking about spiritual growth and reflecting on what it means to be an integral human being. We were committed to pushing each other forward, and for both of us, our evolutionary progress was more important than our relationship itself. For us, our development was the purpose of our relationship; the context in which it played itself out. At times we were intimately close, but then we would each go our own way again and disappear into the mystery of traveling. Then, often surprisingly, we would meet each other again, and endlessly discuss our adventures and realizations. We would never let each other off the hook and would constantly address those sides of ourselves that we feared to confront or were ashamed to admit, for they were too painful... or too beautiful.

One day we were hanging out together on Haad Rin Beach in Thailand, deeply engaged in a conversation about the nature of the masculine and the feminine, and how their dynamics expressed themselves in relationships. It was obvious to both of us that I had a typically masculine problem. I overemphasized freedom, whereas commitment was intimidating to me. By that time, Aloka wanted more than just a casual relationship, but the thought alone already scared me. I immediately felt confined, just imagining the whole notion of exclusive relationships. I had just managed to break free from my societal imprint; was utterly in love with my lifestyle of traveling the globe freely; and was enjoying an inner life of expansion into being. In my mind a committed relationship would be like a new cage. It would threaten everything I had just gained. I was convinced that such a formula would mean losing access to the rich diversity life had to offer, and that it would constrain the free flow of my life force once again. Yet at the same time I also wanted to stay in relationship with Aloka, as I deeply valued the preciousness of what we had together. I wanted it both ways, and not surprisingly, this created tensions between us. I didn't feel ready to fully commit, for I could see that—even though I had come a long way in healing myself psychologically—when it came to women, I still wasn't free. I felt energetically inhibited in relating to the feminine and was confused about my masculinity. During the course of our conversation, Aloka came up with a suggestion. She thought it would be a good idea for me to go to Osho's ashram in Poona, and work through some of my relationship issues. The ashram was famous for its bold and experimental ways of addressing issues around sexuality, and Aloka thought that spending some time there could be helpful for me to start untying my knots.

Even though I was still somewhat cynical about spirituality, my passion for freedom was strong enough to want to try whatever might help. I truly wanted to confront my blocks, break through my identification with them and heal my psychological wounds once and for all. So, I got onto a flight to India—eager to gain more clarity about my relationship with the feminine, women and my own masculinity.

4

Incidents of Nothingness

It was clear that I had left the domain of psychology behind as my exclusive focus and I had entered into the new uncharted territory of spirituality. My space of silence had expanded further, and with that my heart had opened up more. The quality of the writings in my diary started to change as well. From pure psychological self-analysis, more poetic descriptions of the beauty and magic around me started to emerge. I became intoxicated with the wonders of life and the sheer mystery of my own existence.

"OSHO SAID THAT ONLY WHITE ROBES ARE permitted for attending the evening meetings." I had just arrived at the Poona ashram. My kind but eager host introduced me to the ashram rules. It struck me that he prefaced almost everything he uttered with: "Osho said..." I couldn't grasp why he wouldn't speak his own mind. My cynicism about ashrams and gurus kicked in again. If his well-intended explanations were anywhere near indicative of what ashram life was really like, for sure I wouldn't last long in this place. The only thing I was able to hear behind his expressions of devotional submission to the master's word was a lack of self-responsibility. I had always disliked communes, or groups of people pursuing the same agenda, and had always been critical of the politics and power games that I believed inevitably follow from such social constructions. Why didn't these people think for themselves? Why did they blindly follow the guru and his system? I sensed tightness and inauthenticity in their attitude. Had I landed in another social group in which people gave up on their integrity as individuals for the sake of belonging to a bigger whole? Where did this need to create intimacy with others through a set of shared ideas come from? This was exactly what I had fought so hard against when I ripped myself away from the confining powers of my Israeli conditioning. To me, uncritical and unconscious compliance with any type of group conditioning was simply a way to avoid facing our real condition of existential aloneness; a way to soothe the anxiety that always lingers in the background of our awareness because of our innate sense of separateness.

Many of the ashram's rituals and habits were off-putting to me. I didn't like the white robe ceremony, celebrating the holy persona of the guru and honoring his empty chair. I disliked the peaceful looks of holiness on people's faces as they walked out of the samadhi room. I saw it all as too serious and artificially important. I wanted to relate to life in an uncomplicated way. To me, ashram culture was about favoring a social self-image above the naturalness of life, and allowing it to suppress the delicate reality of people's uniquely personal nature. I didn't want to fall into that trap again and was deeply committed to preserving my integrity. I had experienced the transformative power of facing my existential aloneness firsthand. Standing in my aloneness had become familiar territory to me—and I had come to feel at home there.

This gave me confidence, and I figured that even in this colorful subculture of the Poona ashram I wouldn't be at risk of losing myself. So despite my judgmental attitude, I decided to stay around.

During the course of my stay, I remained so critical about what I perceived to be the downsides of this type of life that I completely missed the true spiritual potency of the ashram. To the trained perceiver, the place is unmistakably charged with a meditative atmosphere. Yet I was not at all interested in meditation. In fact, I didn't even understand Osho's teachings about consciousness, spiritual life and meditation. I knew what I was here for, and simply kept my eye on the prize. I wanted to address my relational and commitment issues with women and take a good hard look again at my ambiguous attitude towards my own masculinity. I knew from my post-army years that therapy could truly yield transformational results. So, I joined one of the ashram's therapy groups, hoping to find some clue that would enable me to break through my knots. The group offered all kinds of practices, designed to get us in touch with early conditioning and expose the many ways in which early influences, like our parents, had shaped our personality. Days passed by without any significant progress.

Yet while I was busy inquiring into my psychological obstacles, I wasn't aware that a process of an entirely different nature was taking place in me. Little by little my egoic shell was breaking up, and the realities of meditation were seeping in through the cracks. Signs of this mysterious inner process were manifesting in my life now and then, but I lacked the knowledge to understand their meaning or interpret them accurately.

I can still recall the sultry summer evening when I took a walk around the ashram grounds. While strolling through the groves, the strangest phenomenon occurred. There were about four footsteps where 'I' didn't do the walking. 'I' had simply disappeared. All that was left, these few moments, were some footsteps walking the loose soil—nothing more. Unbeknownst to me back then, it was my first *satori*—a Zen word, meaning: a flash of sudden awareness in which the ego disappears and the true self is momentarily revealed as pure emptiness or consciousness itself. Yet I couldn't make any sense of this weird happening and simply ignored it.

Soon thereafter my therapy workshop came to a close. It hadn't brought me the transformation that I hoped for, and I sensed that it was time for me to leave the ashram. For now I just wanted to continue exploring India. So I set out once again crisscrossing the country. I would take long train rides into the heart of India and fall into states of deep silence, just by listening to the rhythmic sound of the wagons rolling slowly through the exquisite landscape. I traveled around in the colorful south, carrying nothing but my backpack. I felt completely surrendered to whatever was happening and had never before felt so intimate with life...

Gorgeous India! No wonder that this is the land of saints and sages. There is an unexplainable sense of mystery in the air. It hits you the moment you walk out of the airport and set foot on its soil. A unique smell tickles your nostrils and you are overcome by the vibrant chaos of this colorful culture. Yet at the same time, something in the air just freezes. A timeless undercurrent is palpable here. It's a puzzling duality that has something very appealing. So, just as it did with so many others, India captured my heart. Life is so simple and rich here—full of contradictory impressions. Noisy kids jumping in the river. The hustle and bustle of vendors everywhere. The colorful spectacle of baskets full of fruits, vegetables, spices and kum kum powder in the many street markets. Playful temple architecture, rich with symbolic meaning. Wafts of spicy food all around you. Women draped in brightly colored saris. The touch of sweaty skin rubbing against your own in crowded places. Chaotic traffic with cars, cabs and rickshaws honking tirelessly, emitting their polluting fumes from the cheap gasoline all around... and in the midst of all this chaos... the white holy cows with their almond shaped eyes, relaxing and ruminating in the middle of the road—unstirred—while the noisy traffic hastily speeds by on both sides. Boundaries are fluid here. Everything intermingles. This magical chaos is alive, and it somehow miraculously functions. It's easy to touch life directly in this place.

By traveling around in India, my senses gained a renewed alertness and my heart melted. The boundaries of my separate self began to fade. A sense of intimate merging set in, and simply being here felt like making love to what I saw. I was sliding into a level of intimacy that was far more embracing than I ever imagined was possible. I had always assessed my own degree of freedom in terms of how deeply I could relate to other people without contracting into shyness or fear. Up until that time, freedom was about moving beyond my psychological limitations; and about feeling confident and strong in front of others. But this kind of freedom had nothing to do with feeling free in social settings. It was based on an expansion of my awareness. My entire identity was moving into a constant contemplative mood. I had entered an extended plateau experience of absorption in being. What I referred to as 'me' was no longer my body-mind exclusively. It was the deeper level of my subtle nature. Out there, in the heart of India, I found out that freedom could be much more profound than what I had hoped for and aspired to.

Compared to the enjoyable state of being that I had started to touch in Thailand, the extended subtle state I lived in now was more mature and more stable. In Thailand I could still trace it back to an appreciation for experiences. After my hard time in Israel my body-mind decompressed, and I simply reveled in the uncomplicated nature of day-to-day experiences like eating, showering, feeling the sunshine... Enjoying these experiences, and valuing them for what they were without the need to add anything to them to make them better, moved me into the now and into the heart. But the state of being I was enjoying now was a further deepening of that young ecstatic mood. It was more about embracing the totality of life itself, rather than just some particular experience within it.

It was clear that I had left the domain of psychology behind as my exclusive focus and I had entered into the new uncharted territory of spirituality. My space of silence had expanded further, and with that my heart had opened up more. The quality of the writings in my diary started to change as well. From pure psychological self-analysis, more poetic descriptions of the beauty and magic around me started to emerge. I became intoxicated with the wonders of life and the sheer mystery of my own existence. And while I was reveling in being, signs of an imminent change in my awareness would continue to appear, becoming more powerful and increasingly harder to ignore.

One day I was walking in the forests near the picturesque hill station of Kodaikanal in south India. The hillside is covered with a lush flora of tropical plants and berry bushes. I reveled in the refreshing beauty of this magnificent landscape. Breathing the cool healthy air here, offered a welcome respite from the scorching Indian summer. A group of local kids was playing in the distance. When I passed by they started talking to me, as Indian children tend to do. When I responded, I was startled. There was just a voice coming from nowhere—as if my head was missing and the words were coming from no place in the sky. It was the oddest experience. It was as if I was headless, and there was just one vast eye looking at everything. I was wondering whether these children noticed something unusual, but they just kept on babbling as before. I didn't know what to do, and just kept the conversation going. I thought: 'They probably won't notice anything if I just stay centered.' But inside I felt like running away or yelling. The fact that I didn't understand what was happening to me made the incident scary. I was concerned that this might be a sign that I was on the verge of a pathological breakdown. Maybe this event was caused by leftovers from my psychological crisis in the army that were now resurfacing. Or maybe it was just some strange side effect of my free and unstructured lifestyle. I touched my face to convince myself that it was still there. Obviously it was. But why, then, had my sense of 'I' disappeared? The voice that was doing the talking didn't feel like 'my' voice, and neither did the body standing there in the midst of this forest feel like 'my' body. Within me panic grew stronger and I made an effort to restrain myself from reacting to the event. After a few minutes I ended the conversation and left the scene as fast as I could. The strange phenomenon stopped. I was relieved.

Out of the blue, another satori had just happened—a glimpse of pure consciousness beyond the ego and the confines of the body-mind. Yet I still didn't have a clue about the real nature of my experience, and I definitely couldn't connect it to what had happened to me during my walk in the groves of the Poona ashram a month earlier. This experience was so much more intense and elaborate that I didn't see any relationship between the incidents—until much later. Yet at the time, I couldn't figure it out. I felt somewhat bewildered about the strangeness of the incident—an incident of nothingness?—and hoped it would never happen again... Days passed by and I slowly forgot about it.

Meanwhile, Aloka had also traveled from Thailand to India to stay at the Poona ashram for some time. I was looking forward to being with her again, so I headed back to the ashram to join her. Two months had passed since my first visit, and my attitude towards the ashram had somewhat softened. When I arrived there I noticed I was a lot more open and less critical towards the whole set-up—and with that, my experience of life in the ashram changed as well. I was more capable of perceiving some of its gifts and taking them in. This time I could sense the spiritual richness of the place, and it became clear to me that many people living there had an authentic love and appreciation for life. In fact, their way of relating to life greatly resembled my own ideals. Many of the sannyasins were open and loving, and their lifestyle gave me confidence that I could open up more too. I felt safe and accepted in the ashram and experienced a depth of human connection that I had always longed for. In this supportive atmosphere my resolve to address my lack of clarity about relationships, masculinity and the feminine moved to the foreground again.

The Poona ashram is famous for its wild dance parties and its promotion of sexual freedom. The ashram had set up a unique culture which enabled its residents to experience, befriend and explore the intricate area of sexuality. It was a great place to decompress the body-mind and release all sorts of sexual-emotional repressions—and it clearly catered to a need...

For many people coming from conventional culture, sexuality had turned into a shadow issue, at least to one degree or another. Often, the way we handle our sexual-emotional energy is tied up with some form of reactivity. We may repress it, alienate it, deny it, project it onto others, over-indulge in it, dramatize it... the range of defense strategies that can get mixed up with this primal force is elaborate; and trying to become more clear about our sexual-emotional life can feel like stepping into a

41

snake pit. Most people shy away from such an endeavor altogether, and a healthy, straightforward and clear relationship to their sexual-emotional reality is more the exception than the rule.

It was no different for me. Despite all the wonderful breakthroughs and real changes that had taken place in me, I was still essentially locked up behind my virtual wall. I could intuitively sense that my disconnection from my masculine strength, my pattern of withdrawal, my fear of social settings, and my sense of feeling separated from life, were all somehow connected to one other—like one big cluster, waiting to be unraveled.

Both Aloka and I wanted to get to the bottom of our particular repressions and took a deep dive into the colorful subculture of ashram life. We frequented the ashram parties, and danced the night away to the beat of the trance music. The freedom to be crazy was liberating. I noticed how beneficial it was for the human body and how it freed up, reorganized and replenished the body's energy systems.

In the midst of this life-positive climate of sexual freedom and emotional openness, it began to dawn on me that just partaking in the buzz of ashram life was not enough. Something more profound was required. I realized that no matter how crazy or far-out my exterior activities might get, nothing I tried would deliver me the hoped-for result, unless it was supported by a deep, energetic rootedness in my own presence. I realized that if I truly wanted to unravel the cluster of shadow voices that I had carried along since childhood, I needed to dive deep, examine my inner world up close and cultivate a deeper presence.

With that realization, my curiosity about starting practicing formal meditation grew. Because I didn't have a clue what traditional meditation was all about, Aloka bought me a book in which Osho described different types of meditation. The only type that attracted me was *shikantaza*: 'just sitting'. I started practicing. Twice a day I used to go to the samadhi room—the room where Osho used to live. The place was air-conditioned, and the atmosphere in it was deeply silent. I loved to meditate there.

42

In the beginning I used to sit down and wait for something special to happen. But nothing ever happened, so I quickly gave up my sense of anticipation and just sat there, feeling really nice and calm. It was intensely enjoyable. My meditation routine didn't require much effort for me. I didn't have a noisy mind, and my awareness was already deeply meditative at that point—even though I didn't realize it.

Slowly but surely, my ashram routine fell into shape: I meditated in silence during the day and danced in ecstasy during the night. Life was rich here. All of it was centered around integrating psychology and spirituality—'Freud and Buddha', as the saying goes. It was dedicated to exploring the contents of the mind, as well as to transcending the mind altogether. Both these dimensions of the human being were given equal opportunity for growth here.

Little by little the mutually enriching effects of addressing both aspects began showing themselves in me. I felt more and more rooted in my own presence, connected to my masculinity, and intimate with life. Meanwhile, my relationship with Aloka had also shifted gears, and even all the gorgeous women for which the ashram was famous didn't distract me from my bond with her. But even though life in the ashram was inspiring, it was also isolated from society and the wider culture. I could see how easily this wonderful communal spirit could be lived in a protected environment—within this meditative atmosphere and between people with similar intentions—but what I really wanted, was to be able to live this quality of freedom everywhere. I wanted to take it with me, outside of the boundaries of this juicy subculture.

Soon springtime came and Poona was getting hot. Aloka and I decided to head towards the north of India and travel around there. I was now three years into my travels and still felt good about the way I was going about my life. I still wanted life's river to carry me wherever it would and had no thoughts nor plans for the future. My Israeli friends saw me as a lost case and always made sure to tell me things like: "Nothing you try is going to help you. You will always stay an Israeli." Most of them by now had found their place within Israeli society, and from their perspective, people like me were escaping reality and occupying themselves with meaningless pursuits. But despite their disapproving attitude, my resolve was unwavering. The over-all directional force of my life process was simply too overwhelming. I was hypnotized by the extraordinary sense of freedom, the lively intimacy and the captivating silence I was living in.

When we arrived in New Delhi I bought myself an old Royal Enfield Bullet motorcycle and we drove deeper into the north of India. We made a stop in Rishikesh to attend a yoga retreat and then headed to Manali—a hill station in the mountains of Himachal Pradesh. Driving that heavy motorbike into the curvy roads of the Indian Himalayas, riding slowly in fourth gear, generated an overwhelming sense of symbiotic oneness with the environment. The hypnotic sound of the piston rattling up and down threw me into a meditative mood. I felt one with the beautiful wild nature around me. The felt sense of intimacy with my surroundings was almost unbearable. As if there were no barriers, no difference—complete exposure. My consciousness expanded and my mind became completely empty—thoughtless for long periods of time.

From Manali we headed to Ladakh. The drive through the desolate lunar landscape of the Tibetan plateau was breathtakingly beautiful. Lonely roads reaching ever further into the vast open space; rugged plains as far as the eye could see, only interrupted by the holy shapes of ancient Buddhist stupas rising up here and there. It is said that the form of the stupa is designed to convey the stillness of the enlightened Buddha Mind. Whatever the actual effects of the sight of these intriguing structures might be, one thing was obvious to me: The unique beauty of this environment and the vastness of this untamed natural landscape powerfully supported and reinforced my own inner stillness. The Ladakh area compelled me to marvel at its enchanting beauty. Tibetan culture is still very much alive here. Age-old Buddhist monasteries and colorful Tibetan prayer flags adorn the mesmerizing landscape. Majestic mountain peaks and glaciers cast a hypnotic spell of timelessness and tranquility on the mind. An unparalleled sense of serenity saturates the air. Nature's silence is eloquent here.

So, when we arrived in Ladakh, I felt like staying there forever. Aloka stayed with me for some time, but then took off to Dharamsala to attend a Vipassana retreat. I drove off a couple of days later to join her there.

During my ride to Dharamsala a huge moody-red sun was setting over the idyllic landscape, and I was riding right towards it. The air was warm, but it drizzled a bit, which gave the whole scene an unearthly feeling. While driving, I became enraptured by the rhythmically popping sounds of the engine in low gear. Despite the noise, I went into a state of bottomless silence, and hoped I would never reach my destination. I wanted the empty road to carry me to eternity. I longed for the drizzling rain to drip through my body and yearned for the big red sun to devour me. I was ready to die into it all. The joy was so unbearably deep that I didn't care if I lived to see another day. This moment was full. It contained all I ever needed.

When I arrived in Dharamsala, I joined the Vipassana retreat. I was curious and wanted to learn how to meditate. When I joined the group for my first meditation session I sat for two hours straight, barely noticing the passage of time. The rigorous meditation schedule of this ten-day retreat was easy for me. I heard others talk, and even complain, about the pains and challenges of sitting still for such long stretches of time; and I wondered why these long periods went by completely effortlessly for me. Did I do it the wrong way? Maybe I just didn't get how I was supposed to meditate? I was unaware at the time that I was already living in a deeply contemplative state all the time. Being in the strict settings of a formal meditation retreat or driving my noisy Enfield motorcycle didn't make much difference to my inner state. There was deep silence, irrespective of the circumstances.

Still, I couldn't figure out what was happening to me, and I constantly asked myself: Is all of this real, or is it just a byproduct of the joy of traveling? I didn't have a clue. My relationship with people was so beautiful. I was so open and receptive. It all seemed like a fairy tale—too good to be true. My mind couldn't grasp it and tried to put it down as a romantic illusion, triggered by exotic traveling.

After some consideration, I figured that the only way to find out what was really going on, would be to remove the presumed trigger, leave gorgeous India, and see whether my state of being would continue to hold. I decided to go back to Israel, and expose myself once again to the environment in which it had all begun. I was curious to find out whether the silence, intimacy and spaciousness that had become so powerfully present in me during my years in India would still last under conditions that had always pushed my buttons. With slight nervousness and a lot of anticipation I boarded a plane back to Tel-Aviv. It had been six years since I was last there.

5

My First Priority

*I began to see that freedom could mean a lot more than
just the absence of psychological obstacles. Alongside
psychological freedom, there was something like spiritual
freedom as well—and this freedom could be found in the
intimacy of our own depth, where the mind has fallen silent.*

D URING THE FIRST FEW DAYS IN ISRAEL, SOME
small but meaningful matters caught my attention. It started
the moment I landed in Tel-Aviv and walked through the
airport to pick up my luggage. I noticed right away that the Hebrew
characters on the signposts, and the sounds of the Hebrew language did
not conjure up any special sense of being home. Even though Hebrew
was obviously still my native tongue, it only felt superficially familiar. It
no longer brought up any associations with our characteristic collective
identity in me, nor did it evoke the typical emotional atmosphere of the
Israeli mindset any longer, as it always had. The language didn't mean
anything more than what it was literally meant to refer to—as if only its
signs and sounds applied to me, but the story behind them no longer
held true.

As the days went by, I also noticed that I no longer felt agitated by
the constant honking of the cars in Tel-Aviv city. That annoying noise
had always represented Israeli aggression to me. It used to make me feel
contracted and confined. Now, I couldn't see even the slightest response
to it. The honking no longer carried any meaning to me. It was simply
registered as the mere sound sensation it was.

As I settled in further, it struck me that I no longer felt any special familiarity with the Israelis. I felt no more identified with them than with people in any other country. Everybody around me here still seemed to be preoccupied with the same collective drama that made them fearful, harsh and suspicious. When I looked around, I noticed the tightness in people's bodies, and the distrust in their eyes. Their identification with the Israeli psyche still seemed to keep pulling their strings, whereas I felt as if my ties to that source had been severed. As a result, I had a wonderful time here. I was simply enjoying what my native culture had to offer, without feeling confined. I delighted in the vibrant atmosphere, the warmth, the great food, the love for life, and the non-concealing directness that was so characteristic here. I realized that my reactivity to the Israeli mindset was gone: The umbilical cord to my cultural conditioning had been cut.

But what excited me the most, during the months that followed, was that my sense of silence, intimacy and fullness remained untouched. It was equally as strong right in the midst of noisy Tel-Aviv, pushing on every possible button of my previous sensitivities, as it was while riding my motorcycle in the Himalayas, or enjoying the long train rides deep into the heart of India. Even when confronted with the fire of the Israeli spirit, my inner quietude still remained intact. It was not merely the fleeting byproduct of carelessly traveling around in exotic places. It had become part of me—and I carried it with me wherever I went. This truly felt liberating. I was no longer so given over to the whims of external circumstances. A mysterious inner silence had taken residence in my heart. It felt deeper and richer than just some state of psychological balance or emotional equanimity—and it began to dawn on me that this had to be a spiritual opening of some sort. It felt as if my awareness had expanded beyond the mind, and this expansion had widened my sense of freedom. Up until this point I had always understood freedom to be psychological freedom. Now, I began to see that freedom could mean a lot more than just the absence of psychological obstacles. Alongside psychological freedom, there was something like spiritual freedom as well—and this freedom could be found in the intimacy of our own depth, where the mind has fallen silent.

Little by little I began to sense the enormous possibilities in pursuing both forms of freedom. I could feel the pull of emerging potentials, still lying ahead of me. It was exciting, and I wanted to pursue them all. Everything else seemed superfluous. It all paled in comparison with the bright promise of a more integral liberation; one that would include the psychological as well as the spiritual dimension of my own being. That summer I made a firm resolve: 'Liberation is my first priority now. I am devoting the rest of my life to it.'

I decided to head back to the Poona ashram because I found it to be a great place where both psychological and spiritual growth received their due attention. I wanted to enroll in a month-long group therapy course. This course would use a method called 'pulsation' which was developed by Wilhelm Reich—a student of Freud. By employing breathing techniques and applying pressure on different parts of the body, this method aimed to release the energy of blocked emotions. When I inquired of the leading therapist whether taking his course would allow me to connect me more deeply with my masculine assertiveness, he just said: "Go stand in front of the mirror over there... Now say *no* to your mother." I stood there and exclaimed: "No, no, no." He smiled and said: "You definitely need to take the course! I don't feel much power in your no." He explained to me how this most likely meant that, on some level, I was still protecting my mother; and that I still, to some degree, lived in symbiosis with her. I clearly wasn't my own man yet.

The therapy group forced me to take another good hard look within. It helped me reconnect to the emotional atmosphere of my childhood. It allowed me to feel into the way I looked at the world back then. I relived the many ways in which my youthful energy recoiled in collision with my parents' interventions, and with the Israeli spirit. This released so much repressed anger in me that it was beautiful. I found myself yelling from my most primal base. It was a big breakthrough to yell uninhibitedly, after not having yelled an entire lifetime.

I was overwhelmed by the sheer power and the enormous amount of life force that was freed up, after having been held captive within all that repressed anger for such a long time. I could see how, if my anger remained in a contracted state, it was bound to be destructive. Yet by simply releasing it, it was transmuted into something positive. It turned into powerful but harmless life energy. I understood that this energy was the source of the masculine force, that I had felt disconnected from my entire life. For all those years it had been asleep at the core of my own anger. Consequently, the moment I had been able to release my anger, the masculine force, revealed itself as this radical but innocent power; and all the negative connotations I had unconsciously absorbed as a child, about the masculine somehow being a violation of women, or being not nice or insensitive, were seen to be untrue. The masculine force is simply a healthy, creative life energy that drives things forward and removes obstacles for manifestation. It only turns into dysfunctional qualities, like violence, insensitivity and so on, if it is kept unconscious, contracted and repressed. I had known all of this cognitively long before, yet I hadn't been feeling it deeply in every fiber of my body, heart and gut. Understanding that is merely cognitive still allows for dissociation. The difference between knowing something and embodying it is like day and night. It is like standing at the edge of a swimming pool and avoiding the depths of the water. Once you take the plunge, you *will* get wet and there is no more place for avoidance, dissociation or escapisms.

I remember how some of my fellow participants' breakthroughs helped me to grasp this point. One of them was a taxi driver from London. Throughout the entire duration of the course he continued to hold on to his built-in rigid demeanor—as if he was still sitting in his cab, tightly holding on to the steering wheel. Whatever our group facilitator tried, nothing seemed to work with him. Finally, on the last day, after an exhausting struggle with his protection mechanisms, the group leader managed to facilitate a dramatic breakthrough, and connected him with his emotions. I was touched to witness all this beauty suddenly emerge from underneath his British stiff-upper-lip façade. My own breakthroughs and those of my fellow participants convinced me that if I was really serious about solid results, I couldn't afford to keep standing at the edge of the swimming pool. I had to continue to jump in and get wet.

During the subsequent period I participated in several more therapy groups. My dive into these different forms of psychological self-inquiry made me truly value the healing power of therapy. I was amazed by how easily a simple tool like our own breath could connect us to our subconscious material. I had always imagined the subconscious to be something far off, impenetrable and unreachable, yet it is right underneath a thin surface layer of contracted energy—intimately close to us, and instantly accessible. It just takes some courage, a healthy dose of sincerity and a few breaths to dismantle our protection mechanisms. All the life force that is freed up that way spontaneously reinvests itself in our further growth. What a profoundly effective mechanism!

Despite my breakthroughs during these therapy groups, I still held on to many of my reservations about gurus and Indian spirituality. Yet I was also grateful for these transformations, and I found it important to acknowledge them somehow. To do so, I decided to make a move that was, given my sensitivity to group conditioning, rather atypical for me. I took *sannyas*. In Osho's ashram culture sannyas is taken during a ceremony in which you affirm that you are a seeker of truth. During the ceremony you receive a new name, which was said to be channeled directly from Osho. I was cynical about these kinds of esoteric claims. But the moment I received my spiritual name, I couldn't help but be struck by its meaning. I was told that my new name would be 'Prem Ameen'. It meant: 'sincere love'. The quality of sincerity truly resonated with my heart. It felt as if the woman who was channeling it, directly pointed to my deepest guiding aspiration. So I took it as a curious confirmation that I was somehow on the right track. I didn't use the name until years later. I felt I had to complete the process of healing 'Erez'

51

first, before I could truly let go of him, and before the name 'Ameen'—sincerity in all its purity—would fully apply.

The season in Poona came to an end, and I went back to Israel. This time the quality of my visit was different. It was no longer a hesitant reality check. I felt connected to the powerful life energy rushing through me, as a result of my therapeutic work in Poona. My developmental process seemed to be shifting gears.

A few days into my stay, the same unexpected phenomenon that had happened to me a year and a half ago in Kodaikanal occurred again. I was driving through the hills of Jerusalem and all of a sudden, I was gone, as if my head had disappeared. There were no boundaries—only awareness, pure perception. This state lasted for a few minutes while I did everything within my power to stay calm and keep on driving. I could hardly believe that this phenomenon had recurred. I still didn't have a clue as to what it was and suspected it to be a sign of psychosis.

A couple of days went by, I forgot about the incident, and everything returned to normal. I settled into my father's apartment in the heart of Tel-Aviv. The coming months would be the strangest period of my life. Not only did the incidents return, they also increased in frequency. It didn't take long before they were happening every couple of days. Completely unexpectedly I would drop into nothingness. I didn't understand why. I couldn't point to any link with what I was doing at the time. The incidents would simply arise, irrespective of what I did. I couldn't find any cause-effect relationship between my actions and these occurrences. They would happen unexpectedly, and outside of my control. It was scary. I would be walking in the streets and suddenly, unannounced, right in the middle of a conversation with someone, a voidness would hit me. Only awareness itself would be left—without a center. It would happen with such frequency during this period that my fear grew. I thought I was losing my sanity. I wondered once more: Could it be that some left-over symptoms of my depression in the army were resurfacing? I became so scared that I didn't dare to leave the apartment. I didn't want people to notice that something was wrong with me. I was sure that these occurrences were visible to others because they felt so physically real to me. In my experience, it felt quite literally as if my head had disappeared somehow.

I realized I needed help. Should I consult a psychiatrist? I talked to Aloka about what was happening. She, however, didn't seem to think that these incidents of nothingness were necessarily regressive, and suggested that, perhaps, it was something spiritual. That didn't really make sense to me at the time because in my mind spirituality was about the beautiful state of silence and intimacy that I experienced. My spiritual state made me feel good and happy. So how could these scary and unpleasant events possibly be spiritual? I really needed to understand what was happening to me. Perhaps the therapists in Poona would be able to give me a clue. I figured that, with their background of both spiritual and psychological knowledge, they would surely know about these types of phenomena. So I flew back to India to consult with the with the mentors at the Poona ashram.

6

The Point of No Return

I began to notice some remarkable changes in the way in which I perceived myself and the world. What struck me most was that I no longer experienced my identity with my body in the way I used to....

... The moment had sucked me right into its bosom, without leaving a trace of time. Instead, there was a deep sense of graceful presence. There was freedom. There was clarity. There was simply consciousness—nothing more.

BY THE TIME I HAD ARRIVED IN INDIA AGAIN, the satoris were happening almost every day. I would be having a meal, taking a walk in the park or sitting in a rickshaw and suddenly enter into a state of absolute expansion. No matter what kind of activity I was engaged in, frequently and unexpectedly, I would be thrown into a moment of infinite spaciousness, utterly free from the boundaries of the 'I'. I became obsessed with trying to fix this problem because it rendered me totally helpless. It was like being taken over by a force I had no control over.

The only thing that was clear to me was that there was a big difference between these incidents of nothingness and the silent state of being that I was enjoying most of the time. The state of being was characterized by complete rest within myself, and by a deep sense of intimacy with the environment and others. In being, there were virtually no thoughts, and the ones that did arise were very light and transparent. Emotions were still present, but they felt as if their binding power was dissolving. In the state of being, I was still identified with the 'I', but the identification was no longer so strong that I was compulsively preoccupied with preserving my identity. Because of that, I was able to experience an intensified sense of merging and oneness with the surroundings. Yet it was clear to me that there was still a 'somebody' there—capable of being intimate with the surroundings. During the incidents of nothingness there was simply nobody present any longer. The 'I', or the person, who was abiding in the state of being, had utterly vanished. Both states were of an entirely different nature—so much so that they didn't seem to have any reference to one another. From the point of view of the 'I', the complete dissolution of the 'I' was a fearful prospect, and this fear was the reason why I couldn't relate these incidents of nothingness to spiritual growth. I simply saw them as a threat to the beautiful growth process and the silent state of being that I had managed to cultivate during the last few years.

I was at a loss for answers. Was I becoming introverted again? Was I drifting away from society, just as I had when I was younger? I felt that, with the increase in these incidents, everything I had gained—my inner strength, my connectedness to life, and my sense of masculinity—was starting to crumble again. So, I presumed that these strange states were a sign of psychological regression. Their egoless nature made me worried that I was sliding into psychosis.

It was in this state of mind that I arrived at the Poona ashram once more. I wanted the confusion to end and to enjoy a good time with the people there. But instead, I was completely absorbed within myself; walking around, not saying a word.

When I had the chance to inquire about my condition with the ashram therapists, it soon became clear that none of them had a clue what was happening to me. All they told me was that the 'incidents' I described sounded a lot like a bad dream. Despite the fact that these non-egoic spiritual states were at the core of Osho's teaching and ashram culture, the therapists were incapable of recognizing them as positive spiritual phenomena. I was left with only questions. I grew more desperate, as I felt that I couldn't find the answers on my own. I simply lacked the conceptual tools to understand the subtlety of what was happening to me. Even when I heard Osho speak about enlightenment or satori, his words simply didn't mean much to me. In my mind satori and enlightenment were unimaginable states that would only happen to one in a million. I was uninformed about the refined complexities of spiritual life. My spiritual knowledge was seriously lagging behind my actual spiritual experience, and my lack of understanding caused me considerable confusion, concern and fear.

As time went by, my desperation grew. I became more and more withdrawn, quiet and insecure. It was clear that I was on my own. I had no one to talk to or help me figure it all out. What would I say? That I was going mad? I was embarrassed. People told me that I was roaming around the ashram grounds like a satellite adrift, as if I had lost all connection with the real world—and that was exactly how I felt. The situation was consuming all my energy, and I became increasingly self-absorbed. I was at the end of my tether... I needed to find out how consciousness operated.

In my desperation I couldn't come up with a better idea than to go to Goa—the former Indian hippy paradise—and experiment with drugs. I was convinced that these incidents of nothingness were polluting my beautiful state of silent being, and I was curious to find out whether taking drugs would somehow help me strengthen my state, and as such, keep the incidents of ego-collapse away. I stayed in Goa for a few months, taking drugs and trying to meditate with them. But I soon found out that my state of being remained exactly the same. The drugs neither deepened it nor strengthened it. They only made my mind noisy and inaccurate—creating projections that were completely out of sync with reality. They had an irritating effect on my nervous system and were clearly interfering with its balance. Their only remarkable effect was that, during the period that I took them, the satoris stayed away—and I was very relieved about that. Still, I didn't believe that tampering with the fragile chemical balance of the brain was a sustainable solution to my problem. So I figured that drugs had taken me as far into my quest as they possibly could. I had hit their limits and decided to stop taking them.

I had no idea what to do next, so I simply stayed around in Goa. I enjoyed the exquisite beauty of the place, and the sensuous delight of being alive. I loved the sea, the tropical vegetation, and the characteristic red earth of the hills around Vagator Beach. I roamed around in these hills for hours, barefoot, enjoying the warm sand between my toes. Just being there, watching the rocks, feeling the soil, and breathing the ocean air was sufficient and deeply satisfying. My mind was quiet—absorbed in the beauty all around me. I perceived the stillness in the movement of the leaves of the coconut trees. I gazed for hours at the sky. All of nature's elements radiated a magnificent stillness that touched me to the core.

One day I heard that a spiritual teacher was coming to the area. I was still looking for an explanation for my incidents of nothingness. So I decided to go see him. When I told him about my problem, he simply said: "Listen, whenever these inner shifts occur, just stay with them. Don't fight them. I cannot help you. You must go through this alone... But know that I am with you." Because at the time I still wanted to get rid of them I asked him: "Is there a way to go back?" He smiled and said: "Try it. You'll find out that there is no way back." So despite his less than comforting answer, he at least seemed to confirm that these incidents were somehow okay, and that the best way to go through them was to surrender to their natural course. His advice made me understand that Aloka's suggestion a couple of months earlier was probably accurate, and that these incidents of nothingness were, in all likelihood, related to the spiritual process that had been set in motion in me.

My overall state of stillness had become very intense by now. One day, out of that pregnant silence, something shifted in my consciousness. It felt as if I had moved into a state of complete self-acceptance—something I had never pondered about, nor aspired to achieve. Living in the non-resisting state of being for so long, the sense of self-acceptance had already been close. But it still took a tiny interior click, to bring it to the foreground of my awareness. The moment that happened, everything felt as if it was fundamentally okay. Whether it was pleasure or pain, bliss or suffering—all of it seemed like only tiny ripples in the vast field of equanimity in which I lived. Meanwhile, the satoris kept occurring, nearly every day. Time and again I would experience the way these states of consciousness had the power to rip 'me' to pieces. Every time they happened I was faced with the chilling fear of my own impending death. Yet the shift into this state of radical self-acceptance had created an opening in me, and I began to relate to these incidents with greater wisdom.

I remember sitting in my room in Anjuna, Goa, writing in my notebook that I would no longer resist these fearful incidents. Instead, I would simply surrender to them whenever they befell me. The pain caused by resisting the fear was too strong. Since these incidents happened outside of my control anyway, I had, in fact, no choice but to surrender to them. I made the conscious decision to no longer fight them, and deal with the fear by simply accepting them. And so I did. Whenever satori would arise, I would simply let it be... Over time, I managed to relax into that overwhelming fear. With acceptance as my weapon, my fear finally dissolved, and my interior turmoil was brought to rest.

During the months that followed my life quality began to change dramatically. The satoris were occurring ever more frequently, and I was walking around in prolonged meditative states. It felt as if my self-contraction was slowly dissolving. I felt deeply fulfilled and harmonious.

Aloka came to join me in Goa and we had a magnificent time. The whole area was gorgeous. It was full of simple fishing villages, dense coconut plantations, and Hindu temples with ancient banyan trees growing out of the temple floor. There were playful monkeys everywhere, jumping around in the branches, or resting on the temple roof. The whole scenery was bordered by the coastline of the strikingly beautiful Arabian Sea. The area felt pristine—untouched by modern civilization and fast cash. There was no anxiety in the land, just pure, natural existence—simple and silent. I always drove my scooter here at walking speed, which was the only appropriate response in the face of all this natural splendor.

Whenever the satoris occurred, I would let them run their natural course and be aware of them without adding any further responses. Usually they would subside after just a couple of minutes, and then my familiar egoic functioning would resume. Over time, I grew used to them, and they became an integral part of my life. Every time I could feel them coming, I would say to myself: 'Okay... here we go again.' Nothing in particular triggered them, and I couldn't prevent them from occurring. It was a bit like being hit by the flu: you don't really know how you got it, and you simply sit out your time.

In the midst of this beautiful period, Aloka, myself and two friends were staying on the isolated beach of Morjim for a few nights. The place was desolate and rugged. There was almost no infrastructure, besides some tree houses that were erected in the coconut groves adjacent to the beach. They consisted of the simplest constructions—just open platforms made of bamboo without any walls or ceilings. It was a perfect place to enjoy silence and nature, without anybody around. It was evening. The sun was setting and the weather was windy. The beach had a wild beauty. Wanting to make the most of the last rays of sun, my friends went for a swim. I went running, energized by the winds and mesmerized by the shimmering evening light, reflecting on the long stretches of white sand. Around twilight, all of us gathered for dinner in the big tent on the beach. It was dark inside and only the dancing light of a candle in the middle of the table dimly lit up our faces. We were all enjoying the romantic evening atmosphere, engaged in leisurely conversation.

Suddenly, I heard a loud noise inside my head, as if somebody was simultaneously pressing play and fast forward on a cassette recorder. The high-pitched noise was immediately followed by a deafening bang, as if somebody was slamming a door too hard. The very next moment, there was nothing but deep bottomless silence—a quietude coming from a depth I had never experienced before. It was almost tangible, as if it were made of a physical texture that was enveloping all of us. Its thickness and density made it feel as if I could touch it. I felt as if my mind had just been shut down with a big blast—once and for all. Everybody at the dinner table had gone quiet, as if the door had slammed in their heads as well. We just sat there, looking at one another. A rush of fear engulfed me. I didn't have a clue about what had just happened. I wanted to jump up and run out onto the beach, but I restrained my impulse. A minute or so went by like that, and our conversation returned to normal. After the meal Aloka and I went up to our bamboo platform to retire for the night. I inquired whether she too had experienced this immense silence at the table. She said she hadn't, and without any further conversation we went to sleep as the brightness of the countless little stars playfully lit up the Indian skies.

After a rejuvenating night's rest we were woken up by a soft ocean breeze caressing our faces. Sitting up on our tree house platform in the early morning sun, I realized that an unusual change had taken place in my perception. The moment I turned my head away from Aloka, and another image entered into my visual field, it was as if the previous moment with her no longer existed—it was like a far-off dream; nothing but a faint memory. There seemed to be no continuity between two moments. I was literally *in* the moment. It was almost as if life had turned into a slide show. Each 'next' moment was completely new, fresh and alive. I noticed that all my senses operated in a radically new way. My eyesight had turned wide angle, and registered everything within its scope, just like a video camera. No object within the range of my visual field was preferred above the other. My entire life, there had always been a certain focus on specific objects within my visual field, based on my preferences, or what I was preoccupied with in any given moment. Now, there was simply awareness itself, observing everything with equal interest. The 'I' that had been responsible for selecting objects had ceased doing so. The interpreter of visual data was gone. Choiceless awareness was all that was left.

My senses were now simply registering anything that moved into their perceptual field, without selecting preferences or focusing on objects of interest. The entity responsible for these functions appeared to have vanished.

I didn't relate this interior change to the event of the night before, nor did I share it with Aloka. I just kept it to myself. We still had a few days left before flying back to Israel. Aloka wanted to spend them in Poona. I decided to stay here—alone on this magnificent beach—and join her later. I spent the next couple of days just hanging out on the beach, swimming, eating and doing nothing. My senses were wide open and naturally alert. I felt at one with the nature around me.

A few days later I took the bus to Poona to rejoin Aloka. In the middle of the trip, we made a stop for lunch. I sat down on a bench and as I ate my samosa, I watched the bus driver drape a flower garland around his rearview mirror, as is customary in India. Our eyes crossed and we smiled at one another. I perceived the seamless oneness that was equally within him, as it was within me. It was the same palpable silence that I noticed during dinner in the tent at Morjim Beach, after the loud noise in my head had shut down my mind.

At that point I still wasn't aware that a major shift had happened in my consciousness. I thought I was simply experiencing a further deepening of the state of silence that had begun to set in years ago, when I started traveling. Only later on, when I was back in Israel, it began to dawn on me that something else was going on.

I began to notice some remarkable changes in the way in which I perceived myself and the world. What struck me most was that I no longer experienced my identity with my body the way I used to. This was especially apparent when I woke up in the morning and looked into the mirror. The face I saw there didn't strike me as mine. Obviously I knew very well that this was my face, but I could no longer relate to it as 'mine'. Instead, I experienced myself as merely formless awareness, surprised to perceive itself in a human form. It felt as if I could just as well wake up to a different face every morning, and I wouldn't mind. When I looked at my hand, I didn't perceive it as 'mine'. It was just a hand. There was no attachment to the body of the person in the mirror. It felt peculiar that the less than perfect body that I saw there, was somehow a reflection of me. It seemed so limited and deficient in comparison with the sublimity of my interior state. I remember looking at the picture on my identity card. It was like looking at the ID of a deceased person. It was clear that the ego-construction called 'Erez' had died. When I spoke, it felt as if my voice didn't come out of me, but out of nowhere. Whatever I said or did, it was as if Erez was no longer in the driver's seat. Consciousness had taken over. The self had radically identified with absolute silence. I was simply self-aware as a clear space of nothingness without a center. I was fully in the now. The moment had sucked me right into its bosom, without leaving a trace of time. Instead, there was a deep sense of graceful presence. There was freedom. There was clarity. There was simply consciousness—nothing more.

I sent a fax to the spiritual teacher I had consulted before, and described my state to him. He wrote back to me: "Yes, yes, yes! You are the void. Realizing That is absolute liberation! You are not. Only That is." As I was reading his message, I was surprised to notice that it didn't move me at all. It might just as well have been a newspaper ad. I remembered a cryptic phrase that I had read somewhere: 'In the moment of true celebration, the celebrator is absent.' I intuitively knew that my bucket was full, and I was grateful to receive a confirmation of my state. I was thirty-two and I had realized spiritual freedom; a state of boundless intimacy, love, clarity and grace that cannot be touched by any exterior reality.

Little did I know back then that my growth process was far from over and that my post-awakening years would present me with even greater challenges.

7

Post-Awakening Challenges

*I embarked on a lengthy, and often painstaking process of
integrating my new identity as consciousness, with the nitty
gritty of daily life—a process of further self-mastery that I
have come to refer to as post-awakening development.*

*...My concern about losing connection with my state by
partaking in life was too great. Spiritual freedom was my first
priority, and I wanted to treasure it, no matter the cost.*

THE NEXT FEW MONTHS, I FELT LIKE A NEWBORN
baby. I had to learn to make sense of the new reality I just landed
in. I felt completely open towards anything. Everything was
fresh, surprising, and above all... stunningly beautiful! I saw overwhelming beauty in everything I set my eyes on. This was one of the most
remarkable changes I noticed during the period right after awakening.

Especially in nature beauty abounded. I used to look at the soil of
agricultural fields and yearned to melt into it. I was mesmerized by the
dry, golden corn rustling in the wind. I could watch the grass for hours,
or delight in the mere sight of what would once have been a dull rock
formation. Everything was alive and breathtakingly beautiful.

I remember a simple gravel pathway that I just wanted to walk a million times, back and forth, because the shape was so beautiful. I would
delight in its mysterious history, as so many people had trod its curves.
Every single detail of reality had turned into a song or a poem.

I became deeply intrigued by fellow human beings. So much so
that I began to spend a lot of my time in crowded places, just to look

at people, be with them, feel them, and revel in their beauty. I loved to wait outside the movie theaters until the screening was over, just to watch everybody walk out. What I saw, amazed me: every single person was utterly unique. The staggering diversity alone was miraculous. Yet what was even more wondrous, was that the same eternal beauty radiated equally from each and every one of them. I felt compelled to meet them all and get to know them all intimately; or simply—knowing how impossible that was—explode into a million pieces and merge with their hearts. Countless of the most mundane day to day interactions would move me beyond compare. I would get all dewy-eyed looking over the counter at the cashier in the supermarket, because of the intolerable intimacy I felt between me and her. Our brief and ordinarily practical interaction was deeply meaningful to me.

But the sense of beauty wasn't confined to that which we usually perceive as beautiful. I could see it in a pile of garbage, or in a rusty old bike. Everything was saturated with pure beauty. Inside I felt as if I was permanently resting on a couch full of white feathers. The splendor everywhere was so overwhelming that it embarrassed me. I couldn't share it with anyone, because it wouldn't mean much to most.

Over time, the initial euphoria about the stunning beauty of everything subsided somewhat. It was clearly the result of the stark contrast between my existence as a separate ego, and life as awakened awareness, capable of seeing the oneness in everything. The perception of beauty and gracefulness has never left me. Yet my interior response to this new way of functioning became gradually more mature, and as such, less outspoken and extreme.

After the initial post-awakening period of basking in the wonder of life, with the curiosity and inquisitiveness of a child, little by little, a dilemma began to emerge. On the one hand, I knew myself to be ever-present awareness. There was no identification with the relative 'I'. There was only consciousness, that I recognized to be myself. Yet on the other hand, I began to suffer from all sorts of problems with such very normal human issues as maintaining relationships, making money, and behaving in the world. The old ways of dealing with such matters no longer sufficed, because the way I related to everything had radically changed. All these everyday issues had now taken on a dramatically different meaning for me, and I had to learn from scratch how to deal with them in a way that corresponded to who I truly was. The new challenges that came along with that understanding were manifold and involved almost every aspect of myself. I had to learn how to relate to life from the space of pure awareness, and to figure out how an awakened adult functions in the world of separation, in a meaningful, creative way. It meant nothing less than reworking my entire approach to life.

I also began to notice that some situations still triggered reactivity in me. That reactivity would create a split between myself and life, and in that moment, however brief, I wasn't free. My intimacy with life was compromised. Even though my background reality as pure awareness remained untouched, in the foreground of awareness, I didn't always manage to live up to the bright promise of an awakened life. My primal aspiration had always been to close the gap that I experienced between myself in here, and life out there. I wanted to be deeply life-positive, and embrace life as fully as I possibly could. But to my dismay, I realized that while great freedom was locked up in my interior, I actually enjoyed very little freedom in life. It was hugely frustrating. And it began to dawn on me that I needed to go through a process of integration, in which my background awareness would also infuse the foreground of my body-mind, and its responses and actions.

I embarked on a lengthy and often painstaking process of integrating my new identity as consciousness, with the nitty gritty of daily life—a process of further self-mastery that I have come to refer to as post-awakening development.

Since I had no guidance, I could only rely on my own intelligence and awareness to try to figure out a way to handle the challenges of this new territory. There were many aspects of my awakened condition that I did not understand. All of them were related to this paradoxical intersection between myself as pure consciousness, and my human side. It was clear that the exclusive identification with my body-mind was gone. There was nobody left. Yet, emotionally I was still suffering. Did this mean that there still *was* somebody then? If there was still occasional reactivity, could I call myself awakened then? Maybe I was not. But what was my condition then? It was clear to me that my center of identity rested in consciousness itself, prior to my body-mind. But if this awakened state was really the absolute freedom the wisdom traditions say it is, then why did I not experience this freedom at all times? Why did it seem to be compromised the moment shadow material resurfaced? It was the strangest thing. How could I experience this pristine awareness of untouched beauty and timeless bliss, and simultaneously have all kinds of nonsense running through my mind? Why did I react to my partner in such childish ways, while at the same time experiencing a vast presence that was utterly beyond any reactivity? How was it possible that there was bliss and suffering simultaneously? Pure consciousness is beyond lust and sexual desire. Then why did human needs and sexual urges still arise in me?

At that point, my interpretation of awakening was still very naïve and immature. Because I had no background knowledge, all these observations confused me all the more—and I often doubted my awakened state. It was an agonizing time. I remember chewing on each single one of these questions, often for months non-stop. At times, I felt I could have gone insane. I desperately wanted answers. So I read a few spiritual books, and went to a couple of discourses by spiritual teachers. Neither brought me much clarity. Most of the spiritual teachers I listened to taught that you are either awakened and beyond everything, or you are not. Several of the non-dual teachers who were so popular at the time would respond to a case like mine: "If you are experiencing all that, then you are not awakened." Awakening to them was like pregnancy: you either are it, or you aren't! Nobody really talked in much detail about the rich textures of the post-awakening territory.

In the summer after my awakening, Aloka and I moved to the Spanish island, Ibiza. Its Mediterranean nature is not unlike Israel, and it made me feel at home. Yet Ibiza also houses a social atmosphere that is notorious for its frivolity. This made it a challenging place for me to integrate awakened awareness with life. The contrast with my state of pure consciousness could hardly have been more dramatic than it was here, on this pleasure island full of sex, drugs, crazy parties and extraverted energy. The whole set up in Ibiza is a celebration of the body-culture. Muscular macho men and seductive women parade on the gorgeous beaches. Whereas I was abiding in a state of silent beauty and eternal rest, all around me there was abundant evidence of human ego gone wild. I didn't want to get involved in all of this. It wasn't so much that I was repulsed by the decadence per se, but rather by the value most people attributed to it, interpreting it as true freedom. To me, the entire atmosphere in Ibiza was ignorance and superficiality in excess and I wanted to keep my distance.

I felt an instinctual need to protect the integrity of my state. I still had moments in which I wasn't experiencing the fullness of consciousness—as if my connectedness to it had been blurred somehow. Sometimes it even seemed as if I had completely lost my awakened state—until it would reveal itself again as still very much present. Because my identification with my absolute nature was still not stable, anything in which I could detect even the slightest whiff of human ignorance was perceived as a potential disruption of my state. So in order to be able to keep abiding in the purity of consciousness itself, I started to avoid the scene around me as much as I could. I reduced all my exterior involvements to a minimum, and turned within. I even became very judgmental about what was going on around me—as if it would help me protect myself somehow—almost like an orthodox fundamentalist with a clear, unquestionable view of good and evil.

Yet strangely enough, if I was completely honest, I also had to admit, that there was a part of me that wanted to join this sensual madness. It was thoroughly confusing. How could I be in a desireless state and still have desires? Why did I still experience the usual human desires? And why was there a part of me that was attracted to all this ignorance? So, being in Ibiza didn't exactly smooth out the difficulties of relating to my own human side. In fact, it exacerbated my dilemmas. I felt as if I had thrown myself right into the jaws of samsara.

I became passive and aloof, because I was afraid that my rootedness in the absolute would get compromised. I would simply focus on doing my own thing and observe from the sidelines without participating. My motivation to dive into life with a big 'Yes!' was eroding once more. I just couldn't come up with any good reasons to get involved in this messy human reality.

Being pure awareness, I felt very far from humanity and the egoic mechanisms upon which people operate. I could no longer see the commonalities between myself and them, besides the eternal heart that radiated through them, as it did through me. From where I stood, people's reactions to the difficulties in their lives looked like baseless, futile drama. I could understand how, from their mental-egoic perspective, their responses would strike them as appropriate. Yet from the point of view of pure awareness, they appeared to be unnecessary, or at least disproportionate. The difference between my way of functioning, and most people's way, seemed too huge to bridge. What motivated them was completely different from what motivated me. I couldn't understand how they could take their attachments and emotions so seriously. Feelings like jealousy, anger, sadness and so on had become nothing but a vague memory to me. I could no longer relate to positive feelings either. Happiness, all of a sudden, seemed hollow. It was merely the opposite of sadness, and my state of pure awareness was beyond both. I no longer had any moods. I would simply abide in the silent equanimity of clear awareness.

I avoided people who interacted purely from the mental-egoic level, with its constant flood of projections and subtle demands for self-confirmation. I experienced most conversations as unbearably shallow.

They always revolved around strengthening the ego, or organizing the future, in order to create some false sense of safety. I saw how humanity was living in a trance of fear; obsessed by the need to keep its egoic existence neatly intact. From my point of view, such pursuits were hollow, and it was odd to watch people make such efforts to be somebody, while it was obvious to me that the same emptiness that was me was also them. So even while bathing in all of this oneness, paradoxically, I still felt strangely different.

My awakening had also created considerable confusion, and new challenges, in my relationship with Aloka. Right after awakening, an instant change in the dynamics of our relationship had occurred, and Aloka was the first one to notice it. Because I no longer operated under the laws of the ego, my attachment to her, and to anyone or anything, for that matter, had dropped away. As a result, the whole relational dynamic of projecting expectations onto one another had stopped; the subtle pattern of exchanging conditions had ceased; and the supply and demand mechanism had disappeared. Aloka could feel right away that I didn't need her in the same way that I had needed her before. The demand from my side was gone. It was extremely hard for her to deal with this sudden accomplished fact, and it threw her into a psychological crisis of deep insecurity and aloneness.

I remember how she used to tell me that the man she had once known was no longer present, and that my eyes no longer looked at her the same way. And she was right. From one moment to the next, she was no longer the most important person in my world. The special focus and exclusively personal bond that marks most romantic relationships had been dismantled in an instant. Everything I laid my eyes on had become equally important—just a wondrous display of form arising.

In those early post-awakening years, whenever I would run into Aloka somewhere, it would take me one or two seconds to even recognize her. First, I would perceive her impersonal absolute nature, and only seconds later, the recognition of the personal dimension would fol-

71

low. These did not occur simultaneously, and the delay was noticeable. All of this brought an increasingly impersonal flavor to our relationship. Whenever she made a remark about my disengaged attitude towards her, I would respond somewhat surprised: "What is it that you want? I am right here with you, as I have always been." Still she felt disconcerted, because she could sense my total detachment—and my verbal reassurance wasn't sufficient. She could feel that it actually made no difference to me whether she was with me or away from me. I didn't miss her when she was not around, and felt no excitement or anticipation about the prospect of her return. For me, no time had passed at all. She just appeared in the fullness of one moment, and then simply disappeared again in the fullness of the next.

From my perspective, this was all wonderful. There was an amazing freshness to our relational dynamic, because every time I laid eyes on her, it was as if I met her for the first time. From my side, there was no time factor involved. In addition to that, the inherent sense of intimacy of the awakened state made me feel as if I could relate to her with a presence, a fullness and an availability that would not have been possible before.

Still, the changed nature of our relationship also brought up the toughest questions in me: If I felt an equal intimacy with anyone—which couldn't get any deeper—then what exactly was so special about my relationship with her? If the depth of intimacy I felt with her was no more profound than the intimacy I felt with the cleaning lady in the hall, wouldn't it be more authentic, then, to step out of the boundaries of this relationship, rather than continue to play out some fictitious role of exclusivity? What was the exact nature of the personal bond between two people? Once again, I was at a loss for answers. I couldn't grasp how these seemingly conflicting realities could possibly be reconciled.

At that time Aloka and I were running a henna tattoo stall, on one of the beaches of Ibiza. Aware of my need for seclusion, she used to deal with the customers and send them to the back of the stall, where I sat on my little chair, painting tattoos all day. I had no urge to talk to anybody. I would hide out in the silence of the absolute, and shield myself off from the messy world out there.

During that period, I continued to wonder why on earth I would bother making an effort to connect to people who operated from the basis of a different set of principles than I did. I felt intensely attracted to the idea of leaving the world, and living the isolated life of a monk. I even felt an urge to relinquish the body-mind altogether, and die into my own bliss. My fear of death was gone, and the prospect of dying seemed attractive to me. It was like going home, and merging with my own primordial identity; releasing myself into the emptiness of the absolute, where I belonged. Ibiza's gorgeous nature would even make me romanticize my death drive. I often used to gaze upon the landscape, feeling drawn to the moody beauty of the reddish soil in the dry summer fields. Like a moth into a flame, I wanted to merge my body into that red earth and die into that beauty.

Without being clearly aware of it at the time, the ever-attractive silent depths of awakening had conspired with my old shadow voices of withdrawal from life. These different forces were now vigorously co-operating to pull me away from life. Whenever this dynamic intensified, I lost my motivation to continue what I had set out to do—to integrate my awakening with my human side. During such moments, I simply longed to relinquish it all. My state was so blissful and so peaceful that getting involved again in the painstaking process of facing my shadows, and going through the hassle of coming back to life, had lost virtually all of its appeal to me.

Yet, even in my most transcendent moments, deep inside of me, I could still hear a faint voice, whispering messages about a longing to connect to the world, and about descending into life unreservedly... I urgently needed to figure out what my authentic place was in this cosmic scheme.

The season in Ibiza was drawing to a close. My detached attitudes and behaviors had caused a lot of strain in my relationship with Aloka. My struggle with these subtle dilemmas was so consuming that I didn't have much space left for her. She, from her side, had a hard time dealing with my changed ways, because they made her feel obsolete. Understandably, she wanted a straightforward relationship that would meet her needs. But I could hardly muster the energy to be interested in the ordinary ways of life. Whenever I would sense a person interacting from the mind or the ego, including her, I would withdraw. I simply preferred being alone, to immerse myself in the splendor of pure awareness. Many things we used to do together in the past no longer interested me. I simply enjoyed being present, and doing nothing. I fled into my own world. My concern about losing connection with my state by partaking in life was too great. Spiritual freedom was my first priority, and I wanted to treasure it, no matter the cost.

By the end of that summer, it was clear to both Aloka and myself that we couldn't continue in this way. We decided that it was best to separate, and go our own ways. So we broke up.

8

Crystallization of the Mind

To my surprise, it was often exactly during those most trying moments that a breakthrough would occur. Then, I would suddenly notice that something about me was different. Unexpectedly and inexplicably, an obstacle I had struggled with for years was simply gone. In such moments, I knew I couldn't possibly have done it on my own. Something unknown had taken over in the end—something I could only call grace.

FOR MONTHS, ALL MY FOCUS HAD BEEN UPON my interior struggle, and because of that, I had neglected my exterior reality. The consequences for my personal life were nothing short of devastating. My partnership with Aloka was over; I couldn't get clear about my relationship to the world; and I was living with an intense sense of alienation. I was awakened, but my life was adrift, and I felt powerfully divided. Quite a peculiar situation!

Despite all these problems, I didn't really feel dejected. After awakening, everything appeared to be less weighty than before. So I felt quite detached. I even noticed a glimmer of fresh energy, as if life was giving me an opportunity to sort everything out, and start from scratch. I could see how my old life conditions had still been reflecting my old identity as an ego. They no longer represented who I truly was, and in that sense, they had become inauthentic. So why would I want to hold on to them? Why would I feel miserable about seeing them all collapse right in front of me? I understood that in order to stay true to myself, I would have to reconstruct my life conditions all over again, in such a way that they would authentically represent my awakened state.

To do this right, I knew I needed to gain more clarity about the paradoxical riddle of how awakened consciousness, which is utterly formless and timeless, fits into the world of form and time. The fact that all this oneness, silence, serenity, clarity, beauty and intimacy was ever-present only in the background of my awareness, kept frustrating me beyond compare. My root desire had always been to relate to life unreservedly—and so I became passionate about trying to figure out how I could translate all these awakened qualities into the goings-on of my daily life. My hunch was that, in my case, a major piece of the puzzle would be dealing with my residual shadow knots. I could see how my patterns of reactivity were still interfering with my authentic self-expression. I understood that there was no way that the noble qualities I was now in touch with could manifest fully, as long as they were still being hijacked by shadows. I knew I particularly needed to further inquire into my tendency to withdraw. Why did I contract so easily in certain situations, and why did I even tend to retreat from the life-process altogether, rather than engage in it fully, which was what I really wanted more than anything else?

It was clear that my life in Ibiza, as it had been, was over. I figured that it was best to relocate to Israel and build up a new life there. So I flew back to Tel-Aviv, and moved into my father's apartment.

In the months that followed, I began inquiring into the many versions of my tendency to withdraw. I realized that, if I was serious about making progress, I had no choice but to face this tendency head-on. I decided to begin by consciously embracing those areas of life that I most strongly tended to avoid—without holding back. I was keenly aware that in my case, living and functioning wholeheartedly in society had been an area of neglect. So I reasoned that, if I had the courage to throw myself more fully into the societal arena, my shadows of withdrawal would surely be challenged. It would be hard, but there would at least be a real chance for resolution.

I took a first modest step and accepted a job as a telemarketer. My task was to convince people who wanted to terminate their subscription to our newspaper to continue their membership. My attempt was well-intended, but nevertheless short-lived. Barely a couple of hours into the job, I already found my boss angrily yelling at me, reprimanding my verbal clumsiness. It was humiliating. By the end of that first day, I was fired. It was clear that I wasn't able to connect to my power to be out there, stand behind my product, and sell it with conviction.

Soon after that fiasco, I realized that my decision to jump right into the world and take a job had been based on a misunderstanding of my new condition. I had presumed that after awakening, I would be capable of dealing with anything that came my way. I had thought that, since I was now free, I would be able to connect to society, and dive into life unreservedly—and that the qualities needed to function effectively in the world would simply come to the fore when called for by the situation. I had been convinced that even the often less than ideal job conditions of a telemarketer wouldn't affect me in the least.

As I was coming to grips with my failure, I began to understand that spiritual freedom does not necessarily bring along psychological freedom as well. In fact spiritual freedom was producing a very different result. However well I had managed to connect to my power before, awakening had drawn my attention inward again—back into the attractive world of undisturbed silence. I was totally disconnected from my assertiveness, and simply wanted to abide in the absolute, which felt like my true home.

Despite all my good intentions of being out there, the attractive pull of the absolute still continued to support the lingering residue of my tendency towards introversion. The sense of fullness, inherent in my realization, kept convincing me that just abiding in silence was sufficient. My old shadow voices of withdrawal fully agreed with that powerful message and argued: 'Why would you bother doing things like selling a newspaper full of superficial nonsense?' Both forces—the attractiveness of silence and my old shadow voices of withdrawal—kept reinforcing one another, and together they were doing an effective job in undermining my healthy functioning in society. It looked like my shadows were using true silence as an alibi to survive. I was stuck. Life turned into a hell on earth, and I started to become convinced that awakening was a curse—the worst thing that ever happened to me.

For two years, I felt completely lost. I had no clue how to go further and tried all kinds of things to break through the deadlock. My inquiries into gaining some clarity on my predicament were as intense as they were desperate. I knew I had realized my true self as oneness, but what was the real value of awakening when shadow reactivity was still shaping my behavior? Both reactivity *and* a sense of all-pervading oneness were part of my subjective experience, and I couldn't grasp how one could be present alongside the other. Whenever any kind of reactivity arose, I would feel separated from life—and I couldn't understand how this sense of separateness could arise, while in the background I was bathing in all this oneness. I kept scanning my interior experience for answers...

As my inquiries continued, I came to understand that a big part of my tendency to withdraw, and create a wall between myself and life, was due to a repression of my primal nature. For many reasons I had kept a tight lid on that powerful source of life energy.

My own psychological make-up had played a key role in this. I had always lived with this undefined fear that, if I expressed myself freely, my integrity would be invaded somehow. So, from very early on, I had closed down, in an attempt to protect myself against these presumed invasive forces. As I grew up, this inner gesture had solidified further because of the way my parents had related to me. I had often felt as if I was being smothered by my all too caring mother, and repressed by my overly dominant father. In addition to that, the toughness of the Israeli mindset had only exacerbated my sense of self-protection. So, rather than developing into a whole-hearted participant in life, open under all circumstances, I had turned into an aloof observer.

As I increasingly withdrew into my own shell, my primal vitality became more and more subdued. I had become deeply cautious about expressing the energies of my primal nature: my instinctual rawness, my sexuality, my directness, my assertiveness, and so on. The pattern of restraining these lively, juicy and powerful energies had, by now, turned into a deeply ingrained psychological habit. I could sense that their repression was one of my most persistent obstacles in relating to life uninhibitedly. It was clear to me that this would be a tight knot to unravel—and I figured that only extreme measures would work, if I wanted to get back in touch with every disowned aspect of my primal nature. So, I submerged myself in another experiment.

I began traveling to places where I felt people were more naturally connected to their primal nature. I visited Cuba and traveled to South America a couple of times—especially to Brazil, often dubbed as one of the most body-conscious cultures in the world. But even in these places, where vitality, sensuality and seductiveness often fill the air, and people are not shy to show off their physical beauty, the beauty of consciousness was still a million times more attractive to me—and it kept pulling me inward. Whatever was happening around me, I kept witnessing it all from a place of deep silence. I was not at all in tune with the primal energies I came here to liberate. It was deeply frustrating. I felt stuck in a primordial serenity that I couldn't get out of.

In the time that followed, I would try out anything I could think of to get myself down to earth, and into life. I remember how, every time I was back in Tel-Aviv after traveling, I would spend a lot of time in places where the primal energy was very much alive. I used to hang out in restaurants where blue-collar workers went for their lunch break. I loved their rawness and directness, and in their company, I felt close to life. Most of them were not the most articulate nor well-behaved people on the face of the earth, but they had a basic simplicity and innocence about them that many cultured and intellectualized folks had long lost. I was attracted by the sense of freedom that came along with their uncomplicated and straightforward ways. Yet simply being in their company, and tuning into their ways, turned out to be insufficient to truly embody my own primal nature.

After trying out a whole range of things—both foolish and sane—the breakthrough I sought still eluded me. I figured that, to achieve what I had set out to accomplish, I needed some form of guidance. After some consideration, I decided to consult a therapist once again.

In many ways, asking for psychological help felt somewhat out of place, from the perspective of my awakened condition. Awakening was so immeasurably more profound than all the self-absorbed concerns of the egoic personality which therapy dealt with. What could possibly be the added value of therapy for awakening? Why would I make an effort to enhance my life quality, when, from the point of view of the absolute, life is but a dream? I didn't comprehend it fully, but still, it felt like an authentic move. So, I sought out a very gifted therapist, with an awareness of spirituality.

During our first session, I shared my state with her. She was unimpressed, and said somewhat dismissively: 'So, what's the big deal about being beyond your ego? I can see that you feel a bit special about your awakening, but you obviously still have lots of work to do.' Her remark grounded me in an instant. It made me see that any sense of specialness can serve as an escape, and undermine effective shadow work. It had also swiftly turned the premise of my question around. Rather than asking: 'What is the added value of therapy for awakening?', her remark seemed to have implied that it was in fact *awakening* that was quite irrelevant for therapy. Her dismissal of the relevance of awakening for therapy created a sound base for my shadow work. It separated my state from my stuff without further ado, and turned me into just another person who needs to look at his dirty laundry, without making a fuss about it. It reminded me of the famous Zen proverb: *After enlightenment, the laundry!*

As our weekly sessions progressed, I started to get the drift of how to work with my shadow material in a more methodical way.

To identify my shadows, I began by paying attention to whatever was pulling me out of my center, or throwing me off balance somehow. Whenever something caused me to feel a sudden emotional charge, a flinch in my awareness, or an increase in self-contraction, it could usually be taken as a sign that something more was going on under the surface, and that a shadow had been triggered. Whenever such an emotional reaction occurred, I would zoom into it, and observe it with sensitivity and witnessing presence. I would feel into the details of its quality and texture; hold it in my awareness; and embrace it with acceptance. In other words, I did the exact opposite of what our instinctive response usually tends to do: deny the emotion; push it away; repress it; or dissociate from it—because it is too hard to face.

The effect of simply observing emotional reactivity, or holding it in your awareness, is basically that the very act of observing it already creates a distance from it. So, merely observing emotional reactivity is the first step in disidentifying from it. What happens next is truly remarkable... As identification with emotional reactivity begins to loosen up, the energy and awareness unconsciously invested in holding on to emotions is gradually freed up. It becomes less and less contracted around the emotional knot—and it begins to widen. It is in this expansion of energy and awareness that emotional reactivity, and the shadow it points to, can eventually be dissolved.

But for this dissolution to take place with any kind of finality, working with interior energetics alone does not suffice. Reactive patterns are often deeply ingrained psychological habits, laid down as memories in the brain-mind. They tend to repeat themselves mechanically, automatically and unconsciously. So, in order to effectively break through these persistent patterns, the interior energetics of shadow work need to be complemented by a genuine effort to implement concrete behavioral changes in a practical way. Thus, whenever reactivity occurred, I did my level best to respond differently to the moment, and not let my emotional reactions get the better of me.

To complete this shadow process, I also tried to understand the story behind my emotional charge. What had caused me to contract again this time? Why did I always recoil in situations of a particular kind, and hardly at all in others? How did my personal history play a role here? By attempting to interpret my reactivity more accurately, I could often see how the story behind it served as an excuse to keep my shadow intact and avoid taking full responsibility for it.

The weekly sessions with my therapist proved to be very useful in supporting my process of shadow inquiry. Yet most of the real work took place outside the safety of the therapist's room, in the midst of life, where shadows tend to take us by surprise. I dedicated myself to the practice of remaining vigilant about the dynamics of my shadows all the time.

Every morning, I rode my scooter from my father's apartment to Hilton Beach, sat down on a bench for a while, and inquired into whatever it was, at that moment, that was pulling me out of my silence. I would practice feeling *into* it, and looking *at* it with awareness. I would rack my brains to find out, with as keen an accuracy as I could muster, what exactly interfered with my stillness. What was the real nature of these psychological patterns? Why were they happening outside of my conscious control? Why did they arise at all? What was their substance—their ground? I was determined to see through my psychological set-up, and make it transparent. There was a depth, an intensity, and an urgency to my morning inquiries on that bench—an intensity I would try to carry along with me for the remainder of the day.

So, as I went through the rest of my daily schedule, I kept watching my behavior and interior reactions with alertness. Whenever shadow reactivity would arise, I would go through the entire inner ritual again—feel into it; understand it; and witness it. I would keep doing this day after day, month after month, until I had finally exposed the reactive pattern at issue as an unnecessary psychological activity—and until I had managed to change its corresponding behavior as well.

During the years that followed, shadow work was the main focus of my life, and as my self-inquiries progressed, I became more and more familiar with the topography of my own inner landscape. I began to better understand the patterns of my emotions. But I also became aware of the ways in which my shadow reactivity affected my state of consciousness.

During that time, I noticed that my attention moved like the zoom lens of a camera. It was rooted in the absolute, yet from that 'position' it kept moving back and forth from absolute to relative. Sometimes, my attention was so deeply absorbed in the absolute that the manifest world seemed like nothing but a negligible speck of dust. At other times, my absorption in the absolute was compromised by shadow voices, demanding to be heard. In such moments, my attention got entangled in the relative dimension of my existence again. It became temporarily distracted from the beauty of pure silence; and it was sucked back into the quagmire of my left-over neurosis.

Yet, even though my attention would fluctuate between absolute and relative, the basic identification with the mind and the ego, as I had known it before awakening, never returned. Whenever I felt as if I had lost the awakened state because of emotional reactivity, I was always able to move my attention back to the state of pure awareness and recognize my identity as the absolute again. Awakened awareness was always present in the background, yet it would require a subtle effort of my attention to recognize it all the time. During my first few post-awakening years, realization had not yet become spontaneously permanent and stable.

The fact that emotional reactivity continued to create moments in which I forgot about my true nature, kept me highly motivated to engage in shadow work. Still, working with shadows, and habitual repressions, was never easy. Some of them were part of the very foundation of my personality. These deep shadow knots were the hardest ones to untie. Many a time, I couldn't even identify them clearly. When I had finally figured out what the obstacle was, I would often have to go through prolonged periods of inner struggle, during which I did not succeed in staying open, clear, and present with the issue.

I remember how I would do all I could to break through some particular shadow knot. I would watch the contraction arise, feel into its texture, bring witnessing presence to it in order to dis-identify from it, and then try to alter my behavioral responses. But despite all my efforts, reactivity would still overtake me, tainting the clarity of my awareness, and making me feel helpless and discouraged. At times, shadow work felt like pulling my leg out of a mold of fully set concrete. It just seemed impossible. Still, even when I couldn't see any way out, I would just keep trying against all odds. My freedom was too precious to me, and I wanted to pursue it, no matter what.

To my surprise, it was often exactly during those most trying moments that a breakthrough would occur. Then, I would suddenly notice that something about me was different. Unexpectedly and inexplicably, an obstacle I had struggled with for years, was simply gone. In such moments, I knew I couldn't possibly have done it on my own. Something unknown had taken over in the end—something I could only call grace. It was as if the mystery of the life-process conspired with the momentum of my own efforts, to create a transformational breakthrough. Witnessing the magic of this process, time and again, instilled in me a basic trust in life's ways, and made me marvel at the mystery of transformation.

As the years passed, I began to notice encouraging signs that my efforts to stick with the shadow process were paying off. As my shadows were cleared out, I was being pulled out of silence much less frequently, and my realization had become more solid, more stable and less compromised. Gradually, the fluctuations of my mind had made place for a consciousness that was unmoving and undisturbed—and from that stillness, clarity had emerged. This clarity was such that I could spot even the subtlest movements of my mind. Whenever the tiniest flinch announced itself, I was able to catch it very quickly—right at the moment of its barely perceptible beginnings. My awareness was now razor sharp, and operated faster than thought and feeling, and because of this, I was able to spot all the nuances and changes in my psyche with immediacy. I could sense instantly when I was losing my accuracy; when my authenticity was slightly off; or when I was not fully devoted to my heart. This new ability proved to be a great ally. It enabled me to spot the signs of my shadow material more quickly and more easily.

Yet, all things considered, purifying my mind from shadows, reactivity and negative conditionings was a long and painstaking process. It was not unlike patiently polishing up a crystal stone. As its crude surface is further refined, it becomes clearer and more transparent. Over time, the crystal takes on a beautiful shine, and it begins to reflect the light more and more brightly. As my mind was being polished up by my shadow work, it too became further refined, clearer and more transparent—and the light of consciousness began to shine through it more brightly. Polishing up anything requires continuous friction. But as common wisdom has it, friction brings forth shine. Because of this principle, I came to call the process of shadow purification the crystallization of the mind.

9

Facing My Core Fear

...it dawned on me that sharing the mystery of consciousness with others, is generally understood to be the function of a spiritual teacher. The idea of stepping into the role of a spiritual teacher was not particularly appealing to me. The spiritual scene, as I knew it, had always been a turn-off for me. I had seen spiritual seekers go to great lengths to leave their old story behind, only to latch on to some new one that, in most cases, I didn't find to be much better than the one they just walked away from. These new stories were often loaded with what I saw as esoteric distractions and sophisticated spiritual concepts. I couldn't grasp how this could be helpful in nurturing what I considered to be the true goal of spiritual life: becoming a spiritually free and psychologically sane human being.

WHILE I HAD BEEN WORKING ON MY shadows, Aloka had been going through a process of facing her own issues. After we broke up, she was devastated. Clueless about what her next step would be, she lived in an old caravan at a campsite in Ibiza for a few months, blaming me for the entire mess. After the initial confusion, she realized that she needed to come to grips with the fundamental human drive towards relational attachment. She decided to take on the issue thoroughly and went back to Poona to engage in therapy. She also began studying to become a professional therapist herself.

As we had both been scrutinizing our psychological tendencies for some time now—me, my detached aloofness; and she, her dependency mechanisms—we felt we had reached a point at which we had managed to take a certain degree of responsibility for them. Neither one of us could truthfully say that our issues had been resolved with any kind of finality, but at least we had become very much aware of them, and had learned how to work with them. Since we both loved each other, we decided to give our relationship another chance, and find out whether we could make it work this time. Both of us were committed to our personal evolution first, and this, we trusted, would give us a good chance. So we arranged the practicalities and got back together again.

My own shadow inquiries were still centered around the different manifestations of my tendency to withdraw. I was determined to get to the core of this involuntary psychological reflex and dismantle it, because it caused me to feel separated from life and trapped in my own interior. In some strange way even my awakened state appeared to be locked up inside of me because of it. This was not true freedom! Despite my awakening, I still felt inhibited about showing up as the person I really was, and I began to feel increasingly inauthentic about that. Up until this point, I hadn't even really told the people in my environment about my awakening. I had only shared a little bit of it with Aloka, my brother and one good friend. Now, I began to feel as if this reticence was compromising my integrity. It was no longer tenable. I experienced an inner pressure to expose that innermost dimension of myself; I had an urge to be fully authentic, and express my true identity as consciousness itself. Consciousness was who I was, and it wanted to share itself with others, directly and overtly!

Not without some uneasiness, it dawned on me that sharing the mystery of consciousness with others is generally understood to be the function of a spiritual teacher. The idea of stepping into the role of a spiritual teacher was not particularly appealing to me. The spiritual scene, as I knew it, had always been a turn-off for me. I had seen spiritual seekers go to great lengths to leave their old story behind, only to latch on to some new one that, in most cases, I didn't find to be much better than the one they had just walked away from. These new stories were often loaded with what I saw as esoteric distractions and sophisticated spiritual concepts. I couldn't grasp how this could be helpful in nurturing what I considered to be the true goal of spiritual life: becoming a spiritually free and psychologically sane human being.

Moreover, nothing in my life had prepared me for expressing myself accurately in spiritual language and being an effective teacher. I had never been interested in spirituality per se, so I hadn't made any effort to familiarize myself with spiritual traditions. I hadn't been groomed by any spiritual lineage to become a teacher, nor did I possess a comprehensive intellectual understanding of the spiritual process. I had always approached my own development in an intuitive fashion, based on silent introspection and sincere inquiry. I had chosen this route because, in the spirit of sincerity, I had always been cautious about any form of authority and philosophical conditioning. I wanted to make sure that my understandings were truly mine, rather than being unconsciously copied. I didn't want my experiences to be colored by the spiritual philosophy of others. I understood how attachment to concepts had the power to divert attention away from the living mystery of the now-moment, carrying within itself a multitude of opportunities for further growth—opportunities that I might, perhaps, simply miss by looking at life through the filter of ideas. So I hadn't read a whole lot of spiritual books. I had always trusted my own intelligence and intuition first, and the fact that I had come this far on my own was encouraging and exciting. Because of this background I knew that, as a spiritual teacher, I could only rely on the force of my own realization and authenticity, rather than count on the state of my skillful means.

However, at the heart of my reluctance to start sharing my realization with others was a much more profound obstacle. The idea of taking up the teacher role brought up a deep old fear in me: a fear of showing up as the one I really was; a fear of speaking my truth in the public sphere. It was a primal and deeply irrational angst. I felt as if I was going to be wiped out, annihilated, or killed, for expressing myself authentically. For as long as I could remember, I had carried around this old pre-rational conviction that my truth was insufficient, and had no place in society whatsoever. I was convinced that the moment I expressed it, it would be utterly discarded, and I myself would somehow be eliminated along with it. The prospect of teaching others stirred up this old phobia with burning intensity. It felt as if I had been thrown right into the core of fear itself. All my other fears—my fear of society, of authority, of engaging wholeheartedly in life, of being invaded and losing my integrity—were but derivatives of this core fear. It began to dawn on me that the many versions of my tendency to withdraw were all in some way nourished and kept alive by this fear. The fear of being killed for expressing myself authentically was somehow at the root of all my life's dilemmas.

Daunted by the magnitude of this obstacle, I tried to disregard my inner drive to share my state publicly, still hoping it was nothing but a passing phase. I tried hard to come up with solid reasons to ignore my calling. But the more I attempted to hold it all inside, the greater the inner pressure became to let it all out. Once again, life had maneuvered me with my back against the wall: I couldn't ignore the force of my inner call to express my true self, but I couldn't ignore the tenacity of my fear either.

To unblock the situation, I began to look for indirect ways to share the absolute with people, hoping that these would prove sufficient to satisfy the growing urge in me to express myself.

I decided to fly to Canada and take a course in becoming a fitness instructor. I loved sports, and I figured that teaching fitness training would give me a great opportunity to work with people and share my love and silence with them in that way. I still remember my first class about the muscular structures of the legs. While I was listening attentively, and taking notes, all of a sudden, the splendor of the absolute took over and filled the room. I said to myself: 'Come on! Who are you kidding? How can you deal with muscle groups when all this is present? Just get out of here, and express it all directly. No more detours! Is it still not obvious that you have no choice?'

So I flew back to Israel, and talked my situation through with Aloka and a close friend. They both basically gave me the same advice: 'Get your friends together in a room, and share it with them first.' And so my function as a spiritual teacher began... I gathered six of my friends in my small apartment and shared my inner reality with them. I can't remember what I said that evening, but the great sense of relief in sharing my awakened state with them, in the most authentically conceivable way, still echoes in my awareness to this day. It was clear that this was the way ahead for me. There was an inevitability about it all that I didn't yet fully comprehend. I only knew that, despite how it might appear, *I* hadn't really taken up the teacher role; *the role* had taken me—and it had done so with an inescapable urgency.

After that first gathering with my friends, I knew the time had come for me to get out there and expose myself to an unfamiliar public. To make my move as gentle as I could, I figured it would be a good idea to start in the more spontaneous, informal settings of India. A more casual atmosphere would definitely lower the barriers and help me get used to the trial and error of teaching. So I went back to Poona.

I still have vivid memories of my early satsangs, as these spiritual gatherings were called in India. The moment I took my seat at the front of the room, my body-mind would go through its fixed ritual. My heart would start pounding rapidly. Fear would rush through my veins—as if the people sitting peacefully in front of me were my execution squad, awaiting the order to fire. It would always take me some time to gather the courage to start talking. Often, when I felt an impulse to say something, I would hold back, thinking: 'Oops, not now!' I was scared of jumping in, yet to my own surprise, the moment I took the leap, words rolled out of me effortlessly, often for long stretches of time. Still, getting started was always a struggle.

The curious thing about my beginning years of giving satsang was that, while all this turmoil was happening in my psyche, I myself was in perfect silence. I would simply watch the entire spectacle of my personality, from my primordial position as pure consciousness. From there, all the turmoil appeared to be utterly insubstantial—as if all the drama was only taking place in the periphery of my awareness. And it was.

During the course of these early satsangs, a deep sadness often came over me, as if all the sorrow of a lifetime of not feeling valued welled up to the surface. Some people in my audience would notice that sadness in my eyes. Still, they perceived the meditative stillness of the absolute as well. My transmission, in the early days, was a mixture of fear and silence; sadness and wisdom. Yet despite this odd blend, it was abundantly clear to me that quitting teaching was no option. The mysterious aspiration that animated me to share the absolute was far more authentic and compelling than the fear or sadness that was still lingering in my psyche. This aspiration wasn't very considerate towards my personal shortcomings; nor did it care too much about my psychological struggles. It was as if consciousness were pushing me to share itself with anyone who cared to listen. In light of this *force majeure*, the only thing left for me to do was to clean up my act, grow beyond my fear, and deal with my residual sadness. The mysterious compulsion of consciousness to share itself through me brought an even greater sense of urgency to my shadow work. I wanted my transmission to be pure, rather than mixed up with sadness and fear. Still, even with these superfluous ingredients present in it, the main quality of my transmission was still the silence of the absolute. It was always unmistakably present. I often noticed how, during satsang, the meditative stillness that I radiated caught on with some people, and how others seemed to be inspired by the words I spoke.

During this ambiguous initial period, I had very little success as a spiritual teacher. At times, I would prepare the satsang room; put fresh flowers in the vase; and sit there, waiting; but nobody would show up. The next day, I would change the flowers, and take my seat again in front of an empty room. Sometimes, it would take weeks before people showed up. At other times, people would just leave, right in the middle of my discourse, and the whole satsang would fall apart. I would just sit there, clueless as to what to do. My presence wasn't strong enough to hold a room full of people, because my silence was still mixed in with psychological introversion. I was aware that my primal fear had to be outgrown before I would be able to develop the presence of a spiritual teacher and to acquire the capacity to hold a group; and transmit what I really wanted to transmit.

I remember how, during one of these early satsangs, a man started to interrogate me aggressively: "Not so long ago, a teacher around here was threatened with a knife. What would you do if your life were put in jeopardy like that?" He spoke to me in a firm, intimidating tone. I just sat there, listening to him—utter silence in the background; fear rushing through me in the foreground of my being. Was this it? My core fear manifesting right in front of me? I managed to somehow talk to him in a manner that created an intimacy with him. It neutralized his aggression a bit, but still, he wouldn't let me off the hook. He confronted me with my other major shortcoming: my poor mastery of spiritual language, and my struggle with accurate verbal expression. He said: "Why do you bother giving talks, when there are so many other teachers around who say the same thing far better than you do?' I told him that giving satsang was my way of being as authentic as I possibly could, and that being sincere is what truly matters in life.

Challenging occasions like these, gave me the opportunity to face my fear head-on, and helped me deal with it. In the meantime, I kept working on my ability to express myself accurately. I wanted to perfect my capacity for verbal expression so that what I shared would touch people, and support my energetic transmission of silence.

Apart from the effortlessness of the transpersonal impulse of consciousness in expressing itself, for me as a person, giving satsang often felt like an uphill battle. I contemplated quitting on numerous occasions. Sometimes I paused for some time, but it never took long before I felt so fake that I started again. It didn't feel like I had much of a choice, at least not if I still cared about being authentic, and living with integrity. Sharing the beauty of pure consciousness, and helping others face their shadows—while also dealing with my own—was authentically what I was all about. So I continued to pour my energy into teaching.

As time went by, I began to feel somewhat more comfortable in my role as a satsang teacher. Teaching was still a challenge, but interacting with others on matters of profundity and essential life questions was deeply rewarding. It created a sense of intimacy—a sensation I cherished as priceless because it made me feel connected—closer to life. This sense of connectedness gave me fresh energy, and I noticed how, as a result, I began to become more engaged with life. Little by little, I was being drawn out of my shell.

Supported by this outgoing energy, I felt ready to follow up on my earlier intention to function in society more fully. I knew that it was time to reorganize the way in which I earned my living, and step it up a notch. I decided to start up a business in Ibiza and hire some employees to work with me. I was well aware that, just like my teaching activities, this initiative would require me to develop qualities that did not come naturally to me. Managing a team of employees requires decisiveness, confidence, leadership skills, and the capacity to create clear boundaries. But I had every intention of taking on these challenges, because I knew that every single one of them would contribute to what I had set out to do: to counter my tendency to withdraw, and grow into a closer relationship to life. So I gathered all my resources, material and mental, and set up a business structure.

To my delight, the business took off smoothly, and kept running well. Every year, I was able to expand it, and hire more employees. Next to teaching, running a business, in many ways, became my second training ground for shadow inquiry. It was another way to crystallize the mind. Both activities challenged my tendency to withdraw. They forced me to be fearless and present, and face everything that came my way with an open heart; and they taught me how to fully engage in a direct relationship with life.

Over time, I settled into a life rhythm that integrated teaching and doing business. I would organize my sales activities around the summer season in Ibiza and spend most of the rest of the year teaching in India, Israel, and all over Europe. This arrangement worked for me, both psychologically and financially. As time passed, I began to feel empowered. I was in touch with my presence and assertiveness like never before. I had come a long way—from a timid presence in the backroom of a tattoo stall, safely shielded off from the scrutiny of the public eye, to an active entrepreneur, working in the limelight, managing a team of employees.

It looked like I was actually getting somewhere in the struggle with my withdrawal issues, and I remember how this period was marked by the distinct sense that some major pieces of my life's puzzle had begun to fall into place.

10

Seamless Oneness

My overall state of self-contraction had disappeared from my system, but there were still pockets of self-contraction left here and there. These pockets were hidden in the unconscious world of my deep psyche, where even awakened awareness could not really reach. From there, they continued to covertly sabotage my life.

MY SUMMERS OF DOING BUSINESS IN IBIZA were a pleasure. The nature on the island is my favorite. No other scenery touches me as much as the Mediterranean flora. I loved to look at the capricious shapes of the ancient olive trees, and used to walk for hours in the countryside, enjoying the smell of the pines, the tamarind trees, the herbs, and even the red soil—especially after the rain.

One evening I noticed that something in my awareness was different: consciousness was everywhere—as if it had suddenly expanded to encompass the entire world around me. Up until this moment, I had experienced consciousness predominantly from a viewpoint that was internal to me somehow. Now, consciousness no longer had such a vantage point. It was everywhere. It was the trees, the ocean, the sky and the mountains—as if a foam bubble had burst open, and the air inside it had merged with the environment. As a result, the division into 'absolute' over against 'relative' no longer made sense to me. Both realities had interpenetrated one another, and appeared as one indivisible whole—which was none other than my own self. The manifest world didn't even seem solid any longer—as if I could stretch out my hand,

and stick it right through the hillsides in front of me. Even the rocks appeared to have taken on a quality of fluidity. There was only seamless oneness—radiant without limitation.

When I arrived home, Aloka and I started talking casually, as we usually did. Yet this time, something was different. I tried to tell her about my renewed perception and stammered something like: "Even though it looks as if we are talking to one another, we are not. There is only consciousness talking to itself." The subtle frowning of her eyebrows made me feel as if I had just been talking gibberish. It didn't make complete sense to her—and it couldn't, as I was trying to express the inexpressible.

The days went by, and my perception remained the same. It began to dawn on me that some sort of profound shift had taken place in my awareness. I had moved into new territory. At that time, I had no idea about the meaning of this shift. The only thing that stood out clearly to me was that there was a marked difference in the way I perceived the world compared to before.

Before this shift, I had recognized my true identity as consciousness. But despite the profundity of that state, I could now see that during all my post-awakening years, there had still been a very fine separation between my consciousness 'in here', and the world 'out there'. As such, my awareness had still contained a subtle sense of separateness—a form of duality—barely perceptible, but present nevertheless. I had experienced consciousness to be the primary reality, whereas the manifest world had appeared to be a secondary phenomenon, existing somewhere in the periphery of my awareness.

As a result, I loved to abide in the radiance of consciousness, and felt utterly detached from everything relative. From that safe haven, I then interacted with the world—as if there was still a thin membrane around my 'I' that kept me locked up in the absolute, and made me deal with life from there.

Unsurprisingly, there had always been some sort of a dilemma, revolving around the relationship between the absolute and the relative.

It had surfaced most prominently in the tension that I felt between the purity of my limitless nature as consciousness, and my limited persona with its shadows. Before this shift, I had experienced the absolute and the relative as being positioned over against one another—and since I didn't want to lose touch with the beauty and purity of consciousness, I had felt that I needed to shield myself from getting entangled in the imperfections of my human nature and the world. The impact of the removal of this subtle sense of difference was so profound that I could sense how my entire psychological structure needed to adapt to this new awareness.

As time went by, I began to notice several changes in the way I functioned and perceived the world.

Most notably, the zoom-lens movement of my awareness back and forth from absolute to relative had subsided. Whenever powerful distractions, like shadow reactivity, would crop up, I would no longer lose touch with silence. The instances of 'forgetfulness' that had been with me all throughout my post-awakening years were gone. I no longer needed to make an intentional effort to find the space of pure consciousness within myself and immerse my attention in it again. I had moved into a depth of realization in which my identity as consciousness had become spontaneously permanent. My awareness had shifted to a level of further spiritual maturity: a state I could only describe as non-dual awareness.

As I realized that a state of non-duality had become my permanent condition, a new paradox began to emerge in my mind. I had noticed, somewhat to my surprise, that shadow reactivity was still occurring, much as it did before, and I began to wonder why it hadn't just simply disappeared by now. How could reactivity still occur within a context of oneness? It seemed like a contradiction. What could I possibly still be reactive against? Why were there apparently still aspects of myself that seemed to be excluded from this oneness? The issue defied the limits of my interpretive capacities; and it began to haunt me... even bother me a bit. What did this tell me about the veracity of my state?

As I kept grappling with these questions, I slowly began to better comprehend the nuts and bolts of this curious intersection between awakening and shadow. At first, I had somewhat naïvely presumed that, upon awakening, my shadows would either be wiped away, or no longer bother me—or at least, cease to infringe upon my freedom. But my own experience now informed me that reality was more complex and nuanced. The nature of shadows seemed to be such that they somehow remained outside of the sphere of influence of awakened awareness.

Shadows are aspects of ourselves that we still repress or deny, and as such, we push them out of our conscious awareness. It began to dawn on me that this unconscious quality was the very reason why shadows remain largely intact after awakening. Everything that is still unconscious in us is essentially shielded from the direct impact of awakening. Awakening transforms our *conscious* awareness in a most radical way, but it cannot really touch aspects of ourselves that we still keep unconscious. Even the brightness of the deepest enlightenment cannot truly illuminate our shadow zone.

Slowly, the pieces of my puzzle began to fall into place, and I began to grasp what had been going on within me. From the moment I had awakened to my true self, my generic identification with the ego had been uprooted, exactly as it was supposed to. But despite that fact, there were still 'cells' of unconscious identification with the ego that had remained intact. My overall state of self-contraction had disappeared from my system, but there were still pockets of self-contraction left here and there. These pockets were hidden in the unconscious world of my deep psyche, where even awakened awareness could not really reach. From there, they continued to covertly sabotage my life.

As I came to understand how shadows are more or less immune to the impact of non-dual awareness, I realized how critical it was to remain engaged in shadow work. At the same time, I also noticed that non-dual awareness allowed me to relate to my shadow work with much more ease. I understood that the shadow process itself essentially remains the same—irrespective of the state of consciousness we are in. First, our unconscious knots need to be brought back into our awareness; and then, we need to reintegrate them into the self-system. But as I looked back on my own development, I could see that my resistance to shadow integration had gradually diminished, as my state of consciousness had matured from ego, to true self, to non-duality.

I remember how hard it had been to deal with shadows, while I was still thoroughly identified with the ego. It was always something of a battle because the ego habitually refuses to recognize the darker parts of itself. It constantly defends itself, and thereby sabotages the process of re-integrating shadow materials.

Once I had awakened to my true self—even while it was still unstable—the rules of the game had changed. My center of identity had shifted away from the ego and rested as formless awareness. From that moment onward, the need to activate egoic defense mechanisms out of self-protection had dropped away, because I was no longer the self I used to want to protect. Therefore, a straightforward look at my shadows was easier, and the healing effects of my shadow work became more thorough. The complication of this phase of development, in my case, was that reactivity still caused me to lose touch with silence, and therefore, it was still experienced as something of a menace.

Once I had awakened into non-duality, that complication dropped away. Reactivity was no longer unsettling because my state had become permanent. The fact that it remained stable and untouched, even as reactivity arose, brought a more relaxed quality to my shadow work. In the brilliant clarity of non-dual awareness, shadows can more quickly be recognized for what they are—sometimes even as they are pointed out. In a certain sense, my darker side no longer bothered me. Like everything else, it was simply recognized as part of the stream of everything that is arising in consciousness.

It occurred to me that this renewed perception could have easily robbed me of my motivation to engage in shadow work. Why would I care about dealing with my shadows, when reactivity no longer had the power to pull me out of silence? If consciousness is all there is, then what was the point of trying to remove reactivity anyway—as if it were somehow other than consciousness?

Yet, no matter how true this all was, the motivation to keep dealing with my shadows did not decline, because there was also another dynamic at work—which was equally authentic: I still cared deeply about a life of goodness, truth and beauty. To me, such a life was the bright promise of a true non-dual awakening, and from that perspective, reactivity *did* still bother me. I felt that reactivity weakened the integrity of non-duality. Whenever reactivity occurred in me, the radiance of consciousness wasn't as bright—as if some clouds had suddenly appeared in an otherwise clear sky. These moments felt as if the inherent clarity, compassion, and love of consciousness itself, were temporarily blurred. Whenever this happened, my capacity to relate to others with an open heart, and to show up fully in the midst of life, was dimmed. Even though such moments had now become brief, they still went against the spirit of my deepest aspiration to live a direct, non-separate relationship with life. Awakening into non-duality had only made the urgency of that aspiration more intense. So rather than undermining my motivation for shadow work, non-duality had, in fact, brought a surge of fresh energy to it. I diligently kept doing it, because I didn't want the brightness of consciousness to be blurred at all; and I didn't want the promise of non-dual awakening to be diminished in any way.

It didn't take long, though, before my readiness to fully embrace all of life with an open heart was put to the test again...

This time it was Aloka who forced me into another in-depth consideration about my life. Like the stick of the Zen master, her incessant remarks had served my personal growth before. She would always point out my potential to me and expose that side of me that tended to not be involved enough in life. And she did so again this time... She wanted me to be more responsible and take initiative when it came to our future. She was unequivocal in her intent and seemed to be on a mission to ground me within the human plane once and for all—with the most powerful means I could imagine. She wanted a child.

We had talked about the idea before, but I had always sidestepped the issue because—like many men—I felt that raising a child would rob me of my freedom. I didn't want to see my lifelong attempts to be fully in life stifled by the demanding presence of a child. Why would I create new prison walls around myself now that I was finally free? But Aloka was unrelenting. Her biological clock was ticking, and she was even prepared to leave me, if I would not fulfill her desire to have a child. There was a faint voice in me that did want a child, but still, it also felt like giving up all the freedom I had just gained. As far as I was concerned, everything was perfect as it was. But then again—what about these faint whispers in me?

I needed to get clear about where I really stood, and decided to go on retreat all by myself to contemplate the matter in all serenity and seriousness. I went to India and rented a solitary hut in Pondicherry. There, I would spend my days in silent meditation, immersed in the perfect fullness of my own awareness. Simply sitting there, all alone, was magnificent and completely fulfilling. But was this really what an awakened life was all about?

I soon realized that my reservations about having a child were nourished by the same old wound that was still lingering in the caverns of my psyche: the fear that my boundaries would be crossed; that my integrity would be invaded; and that I would lose myself in the process. I felt that I had to protect myself against the intrusive effect of a chaotic multitude of parental obligations, for they would surely make me lose touch with my own core. This was the reason that I had consistently dodged that discussion. But was this fear justified? Was it genuinely wise, at this stage, to keep evading the issue?

103

In the transparent clarity of silence, it dawned on me that my reluctance to have a child was actually yet another form of denying further involvement with life. In my mind's eye, I could see the pattern of my life emerge. It had always been about moving deeper into life—from the very beginning. During my childhood years, I longed to connect to the world and to others, but was too shy to do so. During my teenage years, I felt out of touch with my masculine energy—that radical vital force that grounds boys and men in life—and didn't have a clue how to find it in myself. All throughout my adult years, my primal quest had still been about how to engage in life without any reluctance. Now, while sitting here, I realized that nothing would move me deeper into life than raising a child. So, after three days, I ended my silent sitting, left my lone Pondicherry hut, and went back to Aloka to break the news.

The birth of our son—Dhyan—ripped my heart wide open. It awakened a quality of love in me that I had never imagined existed: an all-consuming love that only wants to give. Whenever I was around him, it kept pouring out of me, and into him. Simply being near him filled me with tremendous joy. Yet the moment I left the room, it was as if he had never existed. Each moment—with him, or away from him—remained equally new, fresh and full. So, I never missed him. My love for him was without attachments or expectations. It was pure, free and unconditional. To me, this tiny, tender, new-born form was none other than the absolute, manifesting right in front of my eyes—and my devotion to this wondrous creation was the same as my devotion to the absolute. Dhyan's birth didn't take anything away from my freedom, as I had feared; nor did it add anything to it either. But it did bestow a quality of greater wholeness upon my life.

11

Wholeness

An awakened life is therefore utterly free, and at the same time, deeply human and profoundly sane. I found out the hard way that—even as spiritual freedom is not exactly a self-evident happening—growing into genuine human maturity is an even greater challenge. It had taken me more than a decade after I had attained spiritual freedom to move into some sort of human maturity as well. In many ways, I was back to being a pretty ordinary human being again— only awake, free and a lot more sane.

A S THE YEARS WENT BY, I WAS ENJOYING A full, rich life; raising my son; running my business; and giving satsang or silent retreats. For all this time, I had continued to scrutinize the hidden corners of my psyche, and the results of my sustained efforts began to show. I had now come to a point where shadow reactivity only occurred once in a blue moon. My most obvious shadows seemed to have vanished from my system, and the crystallization of the mind felt like it had flowered into a certain completion.

With shadow it's always a delicate business to make definitive claims. From the day we are born, millions of impressions, observations and conclusions leave their imprint on our psyche. Most of them are non-verbal and pre-conscious. So, it seems virtually impossible to account completely for our subjective experience and our shadows and reach a place that is utterly shadow-free, and where no reactivity ever comes up. I can imagine surprises may still await me in the future whenever I come across some new kind of challenge. The core question, from my point of view, however, is not whether there are neuroses left or not, but: 'How are they treated, should they come up?' What I notice in my own case right now, is that they are immediately swallowed by the conscious presence of my heart.

Other than most of my obvious shadow voices going silent, my lengthy ordeal of crystallizing the mind had also brought about another remarkable shift: it had changed the quality of my personality. I could feel that most of the contracted density that I had carried with me for so long, had now been removed from my personality structure. It had become more transparent. What was left of it, was a fine nexus that felt light as a dry leaf, ready to blow away in the winds. It was still clearly my unique personality, with its particular traits and native sensitivities, just as it had always been. Yet, over time, its basic texture had changed, as the force of identification that had kept it a solid entity had disappeared from it. As a result, my personality began to take on a quality of translucence, and the glow of consciousness began to shine through it. Qualities like silence, love and clarity now radiated through me, and other people started to notice them.

Awakening was no longer just the *recognition* that my identity was indeed consciousness itself. It had sunk in more deeply. It felt as if consciousness had now saturated the cells of my body, the depths of my psyche; and had lit up some of the dark corners of my shadows as well. My body-mind had thoroughly reorganized itself around my 'new identity' as consciousness.

This was exactly what I had been aspiring to: the realization of consciousness was no longer just an invisible interior state, largely irrelevant to my daily life. Consciousness had now touched the more concrete dimensions of my being, including my personality, and had thereby made itself relevant in my relationship to life.

In the wake of this refinement of my personality structure, an intriguing phenomenon began to catch my attention: a new energy dynamic had come alive within myself. It was as if the energy of withdrawal that I had been operating on for most of my life, had reversed. Rather than pulling me away from life, this new energy began pushing me *towards* life. It felt like a passion, reaching towards some sort of completion; an aspiration propelling me towards a further fulfillment of the course of my lifetime. My ideal to be fully in life was no longer just an honest intention. It had transformed into a palpable energy dynamic.

When I first noticed this urge for completion, I began to wonder about it. It didn't seem to match with what I had heard about the nature of the awakened condition. At the time, my main frame of reference of what awakening was supposed to be was a version of non-duality which was often pejoratively called 'Neo-Advaita'. These non-duality satsangs had catchy sayings, mostly taken from ancient Advaita scriptures and writings: 'Life is an illusion'; 'Consciousness alone is real'; 'Simply recognize That'; 'Call off the search'; 'You are already awakened'; 'There is no path'; 'There is nothing to be done'; 'Everything is but a story'; 'The story is a dream'; 'Wake up from the dream'; and 'Simply rest as consciousness'. I knew that all these proclamations were true, because I *had* woken up from the dream, and I *did* rest as consciousness. The realization that consciousness alone is real had at times been so intense that I just wanted to die into the silence that I was. From that point of view, the dreamlike quality of life in the everyday waking state was obvious. From there, life really *did* appear as an illusion. But did this necessarily mean that my newly felt passion for a further completion of my life was also illusory? Maybe the 'Neo-Advaita' teachings—true as they were— only told a part of the whole story; or maybe the simple truth was that there was still something incomplete about my awakening after all? So, I began to question myself...

If I was truly abiding in a state of freedom *from* life, then why was there still a clear urge in me insisting upon more wholeness *in* life? Was I still searching for something? If awakening was this all-fulfilling desireless state of infinite quietude, in which one feels there is nothing left to do, then why did I still experience this passion for life—even for

107

some sort of completion of it? Was this a sign that, despite all my shadow work, there were still pockets of shadow material left in me that I had somehow overlooked? Were these persistent shadows now causing some new desire for further completion?

As my inquiry into the nature of this newly emerging energy progressed, I began to notice that, unlike my shadows, this urge did not feel as if it blurred the brightness of consciousness in the least. Both my realization of consciousness, and this passion towards life, seemed to coexist without any conflict. They even enriched one another somehow. To me this was a clear sign that this passion towards further completion was not fueled by residual shadow material. It was of a different nature.

Moreover, when I really felt into the quality of this desire, it became apparent that it originated not from the mind nor from the ego. I could sense how it welled up from a deeper layer within myself, as it carried a radically different flavor. Unlike the ego's desires, it did not come from a sense of lack, but from a sense of fullness. It was not motivated by any kind of egoic drive towards self-improvement, nor was it animated by the search for a freedom that kept eluding me. I felt that, having awakened into non-duality, my condition couldn't become any more free, but it could become more whole. And this urge for greater wholeness in life—for further human maturity—was exactly what this newly felt passion for completion was all about.

So, after going through another cycle of self-inquiry, it stood out clearly to me that there was more to awakening than simply waking up as consciousness, and thereby realizing the illusory nature of life. I came to understand that, in addition to the realization of *freedom from life*, there was also a vibrant evolutionary energy, insisting upon further *wholeness in life*. This energy can wake up in a potent way as well, and when it does, it continues to drive evolution towards further human maturity—even after awakening. Because its essence is neither mental nor egoic, it began to dawn on me that this mysterious aspiration was probably what some people would call the voice of the soul.

As I became more attuned to this aspiration, I realized that it had, in fact, been with me all the way, since childhood; but I had only intuited it vaguely, and every now and then. It was the voice that had always inspired me to pursue freedom no matter what; the voice urging me to wake up from the status quo. It was none other than sincerity itself, the voice of my heart. It had led me to discover the silence beyond life and death—and was now leading me back into life. As vague and fleeting as this aspiration had been to me before, so clear and undistorted did it begin to show up now. During all these years, it had been blurred by the distractions of my ego and my shadows. Now that my awareness had been freed from these distractions, my soul-nature began to shine through unhindered. It had taken nothing less than the realization of non-duality, and then a lengthy process of crystallizing my mind, for this passion of the soul to become obvious to me.

Waking up to my soul-nature made all the difference in my life. It changed me as a human being. It lit up more human warmth in me; it invigorated my fervor to embrace life; and it fired up my creative urge— reaching out for the new.

In the wake of this life-positive energy flow most of the obstacles that I had struggled with, from the time I was a child, were washed away. My tendency to withdraw from life was transformed into a desire to immerse myself in it fully. My old sense of isolation turned into an unbroken experience of intimacy with everything I set my eyes on. My childhood feelings of alienation were replaced by the realization that I truly did belong in this reality. The impact of all these changes was substantial. In many ways, I was no longer the person I used to be.

As a result, my work as a spiritual teacher began to blossom. After years of struggle, I felt that I had mastered the teaching craft. My presence was strong and fearless. Satsang no longer scared me. I had become capable of embracing large groups of people in an effortless fashion and creating an atmosphere of spiritual intimacy and stillness in the room. It dawned on me that I had managed to express myself in the most authentic way that I could, and nobody was killing me for it. Together with the fear, the sadness disappeared too. More people now started to come to my satsangs, and express their appreciation. Whenever I sat in front of a group, I noticed that stillness radiated into the room and affected people. The transmission of silence was now free from psychological residue. There was no more contracted introversion—just a naturally silent persona.

Awakening to my soul-nature had changed me in ways that even my shift into spiritual freedom had not accomplished. Awakening, and especially the subsequent shift into non-duality, had indeed dissolved my sense of separateness. But it took the awakening of my soul-nature to cause an irreversible tipping point within myself, and actually set in motion an energy dynamic, directed towards expressing my interior state of oneness in tangible ways. This energy's insistence upon greater wholeness, made it obvious to me that, despite being in a state of freedom from life, I still had something to do in this life.

To this day, I still place my trust in the inspirational force of my soul-nature and continue to treat it as my guide. It keeps prompting me to self-express a uniqueness that is intimately mine, and that *wants* to be experienced in this life. Following its direction has enriched my awakening with a passion to embrace life, and to evolve towards a greater human maturity.

I never felt, and still don't feel now, that I have reached my final destination. It is clear that evolution never ends, not even after awakening. The moment you have realized your true self as formless consciousness, the evolutionary impulse becomes fully available to continue its work in the world of form. It turns to those areas of the self that need it most. There, it begins to disentangle any remaining knots that are still preventing you from manifesting the bright promise of a truly awakened life. And thus, it continues to advance you towards the ever-receding horizon of further human maturity.

To me, awakening means both spiritual freedom and human maturity. Spiritual freedom is the realization that your true identity is consciousness itself, rather than just the body, the mind or the soul. Human maturity is the capacity to manifest your true identity as consciousness *with* your body, mind and soul. It is the art of translating oneness into daily life, and manifesting truly enlightened virtues like goodness, truth and beauty. Such virtues will eventually arise most naturally from the unbroken sense of connectedness and intimacy that comes along with the realization of spiritual freedom. But it requires the instrument of a deeply integrated, adult persona, in order to be able to manifest them effectively.

An awakened life is therefore utterly free, and at the same time, deeply human and profoundly sane. I found out the hard way that—even as spiritual freedom is not exactly a self-evident happening—growing into genuine human maturity is an even greater challenge. It had taken me more than a decade after I had attained spiritual freedom to move into some sort of human maturity as well. In many ways, I was back to being a pretty ordinary human being again—only awake, free and a lot more sane.

When I now look back on my evolutionary journey, I cannot help but marvel at the mystery of transformation. What is it *really* that sets inner growth in motion? What makes us *wake up* from the trance of our everyday complacency? What opens up our heart, and molds it to become ever more embracing? What is this secret impulse that gently awakens the delicate flavor of our soul-nature, and strives toward ever-greater wholeness? Is it not all the same mystery?

Somehow, at some point, some mysterious spark—that lies dormant in each one of us—simply wakes up. For some, a time of crisis may do the trick; for others, a newly emerging insight gets them going; and others still are simply touched by an unexpected glimpse of beauty that moves them to the core. But truly *anything* can break the spell of everyday awareness and move you into the unknown promise of a new dawn.

For me, it was often some form of suffering that marked the birth of a new chapter. I always experienced my own limitedness as deeply confining. My sense of restriction was so fierce that I often felt as if I were held captive in a corset of steel. As a response, my urgency to break free was equally fierce. It was a lot like the instinct of a drowning person, gasping for air. My search for freedom didn't feel like a matter of choice. It *had* to be done. Nothing else was more important to me, and it dominated my awareness day and night.

It takes nothing less than this kind of fierce urgency to uproot the powerful forces of identification that keep our limitedness intact. Anything less will simply not suffice.

This unceasing demand for true freedom brings forth an insistence upon sincerity. You can no longer fool yourself. You have lost all your interest in illusory consolations, and you don't want to be swayed by unnecessary distractions that cover up your real condition. Instead, you are inspired by a truthfulness that never wavers—a sincerity that is uncompromised.

Sincerity is the voice of the true heart. It rises up from the depths of your innermost self. Its ephemeral messages are the whispers of your own non-dual nature; an unknowable mystery that is drawing us all back to itself. The quieter you become, the more you can hear these whispers—and if you listen to them with care, you will surely sense their wisdom; and they will guide you into an unimaginable freedom, that is nothing but your own inalienable birthright.

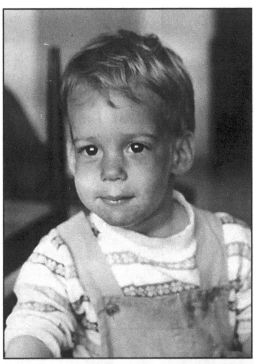

Left: "I am one-and-a-half years old."

Below: October, 1973, Ameen with family. "My father was visiting home from the front of the Yom Kippur War."

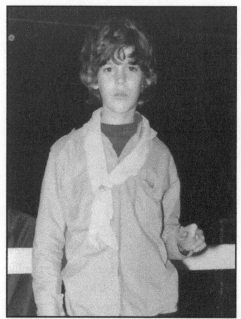

Left: "12 years old in my boy scout uniform. This was the exact period when I witnessed the terror attack on the bus." (page 7.)

Below left: "17 years old and terribly miserable. Locked inside my own cage."

Below right: "On first leave from army training. The worst day of my life. Within 48 hours I would make my first fake suicide attempt."

Top: Thailand, February, 1995. "Reveling in being. The moment was perfect. I did not look for anything more."

Above left: India, August, 1997. "Riding towards Ladakh. I felt as if I was dancing on these mountain roads."

Above right: India, August, 1997. "You can't get any higher with a motor bike!"

Top left: India, March, 1999. "With Aloka in the tree house at Morjim, Goa. The morning after waking up to pure consciousness. I wasn't aware that my life had changed forever."

Top right: India, 1998, "Enjoying freedom in Goa."

Right: India, August, 1997. "Saying goodbye to Aloka at New Delhi airport before going to Israel to face my conditioning."

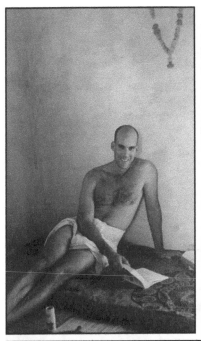

Top left: Goa, India, 2002. "My Indian yogi look."

Top right: Barcelona, Spain, 2003. "With my beloved mother."

Left: India, February, 2003. "My first public Satsang in Goa."

SATSANG
WITH
EREZ

If you seek truth with your whole heart. Then you may be assured that the grace of truth is also seeking you.

Dates: 25.,27., 28. & 30. April 2003, um 19:30 Uhr
Satori-Intitut, Schillerstr. 37, München
Kontakt: 089-54073619, Eintritt: € 10.-

Above: "My first Satsang flyer when I still used my birth name, Erez."

Above: Goa, India, 2008. "With Aloka and Dhyan."

Left: Germany, 2018. "With my dear son, Dhyan."

PART TWO
TEACHINGS

THE FOLLOWING DIALOGUES ARE MEANT TO dig deeper into the themes of Ameen's biography; clarify them further, and make them practicable in your life.

This part of the book presents the pillars of Ameen's teaching and contains concrete instructions about how to cultivate silence, and practice shadow work in a spiritual context. But it also explores the deep matters of spiritual life, dear to the heart of anyone dedicated to genuine transformation, and aspiring to live a life of freedom, truth and profundity. It delves into the nature of awakened awareness; the value of discernment on the path; the impact of shadow on the awakening process; the transformation of negative emotions; the meaning of genuine ego-transcendence; the value of the teacher-student relationship; the role of our soul-nature; the real power of sincerity; and more...

These dialogues are based on countless hours of in-depth interviews between Ameen and Hans Plasqui, conducted over a year-long period in Germany, Israel and Spain.

1

Silence

Hans Plasqui: *A key instruction that runs through your talks is to cultivate presence. Can you speak more about the nature of presence and the importance of developing it?*

Ameen: Sure. Presence is what you actually *are*. It is pure awareness, stillness. It is your true nature. This may sound a bit puzzling at first. Pure awareness, after all, is not what most of us experience ourselves to be. In our everyday lives, we usually presume ourselves to be skin-encapsulated egos—and from that perspective, our identity as pure awareness is not at all obvious to us. So, we may wonder: if pure awareness is really our true nature, then why is this not simply self-evident? If it is what we always already are, then why do we not experience it all the time? The answer to these questions leads us straight into the essence of our condition as human beings.

If we were to take an honest look within, most of us would find that, most of the time, the actual quality of our everyday state of mind is one of restlessness. Very few of us would find an inner world of clarity, silence and presence. We spend the better part of our waking hours lost in thought. We are thinking, without being aware we are doing so. It is as if we have a voice in our heads that hardly ever quietens down. Even if there is no immediate functional need for it, our thinking persists,

125

almost with the force of an addiction. Most of our thoughts are repetitive, random and superficial—most often not creative, original or deep.

Our emotional lives, too, happen largely involuntarily, and outside of our conscious control. Emotions often take us by surprise. They simply spring up because some old pain, some shadow, or some personal sensitivity has been triggered. Our emotional lives are mostly reactive, and a lot of our attention is bound up in petty concerns.

So, looking within, there is no immediate sign that our true nature is silent presence. All that most of us would observe is this continuous, involuntary quality of restlessness.

If we will then further explore this restlessness and trace it all the way back to its source, we find that it is nourished and kept alive by an undercurrent of undefined primal anxiety. This primal anxiety is always present at the core of each one of us. Deep down we are always vigilant, apprehensive and afraid, because we perceive ourselves to be separate entities, standing over and against some 'other', who may infringe upon our boundaries at any time. Ours is an anxious world of 'self' and 'other' in which we feel we have to protect ourselves non-stop—not a world in which the oneness of 'self' and 'other', prior to our anxiety, is obvious.

Deep inside, we are always instinctively aware of our vulnerability as separate entities within this vast cosmic process of life and death. We apprehend the impermanent nature of our existence—our own mortality. We know that our turn will come. One day, we will die. The same cosmic process that gave birth to us will inevitably consume us. So we contract. We recoil in dread.

Primal anxiety is our instinctual response to our predicament as human beings. It creates the restlessness of our everyday awareness. It produces the ceaseless grasping of our minds, compulsively latching on to thoughts, emotions, sensations and sensory perceptions in an attempt to protect ourselves and build up a sturdy identity, able to survive and function in this world. Many people succeed pretty well in creating a well-functioning ego that is not anxious and afraid all the time. They manage to stay in a relatively comfortable state of mind most of the time. But however successful we may be at this, still that uneasy feeling of primal anxiety is always there at the core of who we are. Even when our life conditions line up perfectly, and good fortune, affluence and success smile generously upon us, deep down, that undercurrent of anxiety still persists, because we are always tacitly aware that we can lose it all. Primal anxiety is our most basic emotional environment as separate entities. It is what makes us contract from our true nature as boundless spacious consciousness into a small separate self. As such, primal anxiety is the very foundation of our sense of self.

Our condition as human beings is marked by this cluster of deeply existential quandaries: our sense of separateness, our awareness of our mortality, our primal anxiety and our egoic grasping. All of them are intimately intertwined. All of them are part and parcel of one and the same knot. All of these *together*—and nothing less—must be seen through, transcended and released. Then it will be obvious to us that in the depths of our being, prior to our most basic existential quandaries, lies the well-kept secret of what we truly are—and always have been—pure silence, full of conscious presence.

As long as the knot at the core of the human condition is still intact, we cannot access the great silence of our true nature, and we will remain perpetually distracted by lesser things. Our attention will continue to dwell on the surface layer of our everyday awareness, latching onto what is most readily in its view: to our thoughts, emotions, bodily sensations, and sensory observations. It will remain preoccupied with the contents of our awareness, and we will keep overlooking that we are, at heart, simply awareness itself—free from any of its contents.

Hans: *It is often said that one of the most effective ways to access this pure awareness is meditation. What is meditation, and how do you practice it?*

127

AMEEN

Ameen: The bottom line? Meditation is simply to be still and enjoy your own presence. That's it—no inner fireworks, no great insights. It is just being with yourself in silence—effortlessly. Know that in the depths of your heart, you are always already in meditation. It is your natural state, inherent to your being. The silence of true meditation is always present as your deepest core, underneath the clutter of thoughts and emotions. That is why it is accessible at all times—even right now. It is always right within your reach—if only you would open up to it.

The art of meditation is to let that silence reveal itself to you. When you simply allow silence to permeate you, you will feel full—not lacking, not needing, not seeking. Just your own existence, right here, right now, will be perfectly fulfilling. In true meditation you simply notice that the fullness of pure awareness is already present in this and every moment—and you see that it has always been so. You realize that pure awareness is what you most truly *are*. But because most of us continue to overlook this truth, we need to practice meditation to learn to notice it. Pure awareness is the elephant in the room!

There are many ways to practice meditation. The classical forms of meditation are usually very effective. They have been designed over millennia to help you access silence. But I have to say that I never used any of them. I only relied on my passion for freedom and sincerity to get to my deepest truth—and I organized my life around these aspirations. Little by little, by trial and error, I stumbled into my own ways of accessing silence. And to this day, I always advise people to find their own unique way. In my experience, an open invitation like this appeals to people's own sincerity, which has always been the beating heart of any living practice. Once your sincerity is truly awake, you can trust your own judgement about what works for you. Some people find that some traditional meditation approach seems tailor-made for them. Others discover all on their own how to make that inner gesture into silence. Yet others feel most comfortable with at least some basic guidelines about how to dive into their own depths. So, it is always useful to offer

128

some basic practical instructions for getting started with the practice of meditation.

A good way to begin is to sit down comfortably, preferably with your back straight. Close your eyes and breathe consciously. Follow the entire cycle of your breathing with your attention. Follow your inhalation all the way down into your belly. Notice the exact point where the inhalation stops and the exhalation begins. Then follow the exhalation all the way. Notice that it too has a clean end point.

Following the cycle of your breath will give your attention something to do, other than wandering around, and getting lost in thought. Breathing consciously like this will move your attention out of the mind and allow it to drop down into your body. This will help you break the spell of compulsive thinking and root your attention in the here and now. If you keep doing this for a while, it will clear out random thoughts and emotions, and create a state of open, attentive presence, fully relaxed into whatever is arising.

Know that while you meditate, you will get lost in thought all the time. You might be sucked into some emotional pattern or get distracted by sensations or images. This is not a problem. It is simply the way the mind is conditioned to work. In meditation, you are very quickly faced with the actual quality of your inner life. This can be quite confrontational. Many people who start to meditate are surprised to find how noisy, cluttered, restless, dazed, chaotic, or anxious their inner world really is. It usually is anything but silent. But whenever you notice you have drifted into some mental narrative, or have gotten caught up in some emotional pattern, simply come back to the breath. Don't be bothered by how often you get lost in your mind. Whenever you notice you get carried away, simply keep returning to the breath. Following your breath can be a very effective technique to move you out of the restlessness of your everyday awareness, especially when you have just began to learn how to meditate.

Keep in mind, however, that the breath is just a tool. Over time, you will become more and more capable of dropping directly into silence. As this happens, you can gradually let go of the tool, until it has become completely unnecessary. The best way is always to use as little technique as possible. That is why the more mature forms of meditation are about accessing silence directly, without the help of any technique. Whenever you feel you are ready for this, simply do so.

So, in this more advanced form of practice, rather than returning to the breath when you notice you are lost in your mind, simply allow yourself to fall back into silence directly. Watch the contents of your awareness from the silent witness that is prior to them. Whenever thoughts, emotions, images, feelings and sensations arise, don't fight them. Let them all arise in you as they will. Don't try to get rid of them. Do not manipulate them in any way. Just know that they will also leave, exactly the way they have come. Simply watch them run their natural course. Stay present with whatever arises. If you try to alter the contents of your awareness, or chase them away, you are again using the mind— the very thing you are to go beyond in true meditation. So don't struggle to be quiet. The one who struggles to be still is the one who continues to pull you out of stillness. Let go of that one. Whatever content may arise in your awareness, simply hold it with open attentive presence.

If you keep practicing like that, over time, the compulsive nature, the narrow quality, the contracted condition of these contents, will begin to relax. Eventually, any confining identifications with these contents will be swallowed by the bottomless depths of awareness itself.

In due course, even the quality of primal anxiety itself, which lies at the root of the restless nature of your everyday awareness, will be erased from your system. When this occurs, it is a milestone on the path. It is the point where meditation reveals to you, that you are not the self you typically assume you are; the self that consists of thoughts, feelings, emotions, images, sensations... It is the point where meditation exposes that self as a mere surface layer. When you cross that threshold, it will be plainly obvious to you that your true self is pure awareness, prior to any of the contents cycling through it. Realizing this secret changes the entire quality of your existence. It is freedom; oneness; intimacy with all...

Hans: *You have spoken quite often about cultivating presence in the midst of everyday life, even more than you have talked about deepening presence during formal meditation practice. Could you offer us some instruction about practicing presence as a way of life?*

Ameen: Certainly. Living your life from a steady center of deep presence, is what it all comes down to in the end. Meditation practice is a rehearsal for that. What value does it ultimately have, if you are able to rest as conscious presence during sitting, but then lose that quality the moment you get off your meditation cushion? Life is where the strength of your presence is really put to the test—especially during trying times, when things get turbulent, and life challenges you. Can you still stay present then? Can you still respond from your center? The practice of meditation finds its ultimate fulfillment off the cushion, when you have become able to live from a quality of clarity and presence in every moment, right in the midst of your daily pursuits.

If we are sincere with ourselves, we would probably concede that we go through life not as fully awake and aware as we could be. That is why I always emphasize the practice of bringing more presence into *every* moment. It is like hitting your 'refresh' button, whenever you notice you are losing your presence, and are drifting into a quality of unconsciousness. Since this will tend to happen many times during any given day, bringing yourself back to presence is a gesture you need to be willing to keep making, again and again, in every new moment. To do so takes sincerity, a constant willingness, and a firm intention. But if you carry it through, your unconscious patterns will slowly be imbued with conscious presence. They will loosen their grip on you, and gradually disappear. To me, such a moment-to-moment practice is one of the single most valuable practice instructions you can live by.

For many people, however, the most potent way to cultivate silence turns out to be some combination of daily meditation periods, and the moment-to-moment practice of touching in with your own core and returning to a state of presence. The longer meditation periods will gradually deepen your capacity for presence, whereas the little moments here and there will train your ability to shift fluently from mind to silence.

Alongside these general ways to practice, there are also more concrete ways to optimize your quality of presence in your life. You may find, for example, that some activities will be conducive for aligning yourself with the silence that you are, whereas others, by nature, will trigger a more restless quality in you. If you want your everyday life to be permeated by a deeper quality of presence, it is imperative to find out what supports the move into presence in your own case.

For some people, spending time in nature and enjoying its silence, helps them attune to their own silence. For others, being close to people who have realized this silence works best. Still others greatly benefit from practices like martial arts and certain forms of yoga because these disciplines teach you how to let go, *and* still be vigilant at the same time. Literally anything could serve as a meditative practice, because mediation is your natural state. It could be as simple as sitting on a bench for a while, taking a walk in the park, lying on the beach, or listening to music...

I found out early on that, for myself, all kinds of physical body practices were very effective in connecting me to a quality of presence. I have always loved sports. During my younger years, I used to surf the ocean, go to the gym, and lift weights. Now, I still practice yoga and running—and lately, I added swimming. The effect of such physical activities is not unlike following the breathing cycle during formal meditation. Investing attention in the body moves that attention out of the mind. As a result, compulsive mental-emotional processes subside. The mind clears and falls silent. A quality of spaciousness and clarity sets in, and presence deepens.

Different bodily practices have their own unique effect. Yogic postures, for example, replenish the body and keep it open and relaxed. They allow your vital energies to flow freely, and prevent bodily tensions from building up. Physical practices, especially those designed to build up muscles, like weightlifting, generate an abundance of life energy, which makes you feel physically vibrant. But the bottom line of any such practices is that they produce a strong and healthy body—and this naturally creates more space to really be present in life.

For me, it was probably running that was the most effective. I always experienced running as a deeply meditative activity. Regardless of the quality of my day, the moment I started running, and the rhythm of my footsteps synchronized with my breathing, my presence strengthened. My clarity of mind increased, and a sense of freedom kicked in. Even after awakening, running continued to serve me well—especially during the time that I was trying to make sense of my state. I remember how, whenever I was in the midst of dealing with some shadow knot, running often brought me the necessary clarity and centeredness to break through it. Even while I was struggling to come to terms with my powerful longing to withdraw from life altogether, and merge into the unconditional freedom of pure awareness, running linked me up with the body, again and again. It played a major role in helping me integrate my new-found state with life.

But it was also more than just a way to process things. It was a way to express the inner freedom my new-found state had disclosed to me. Right after awakening, I felt as if I was plugged into a boundless source of energy. There was so much energy coursing through my system that I *had* to run. I never ran as much as I did back then. Running for hours was my way of embodying my inner sense of limitlessness and spaciousness. It was a celebration of the joy of living in freedom, and my love for life. Everywhere I traveled, I used to go running for long stretches of time, often in nature. It was marvelous... Only the sound of my footsteps, my breathing... and the silence of nature moving into communion with my own silence.

133

Hans: *Another way to cultivate silence that you often speak about is to come to terms with our existential aloneness. Facing our aloneness is an especially important part of your teaching. What do you mean by aloneness, and wherein lies the transformational power of being aware of it?*

Ameen: If we look carefully into the workings of our minds, we will be surprised to notice how much energy and attention we spend reaching outward, towards others and objects around us, and creating attachments to them. There is a built-in mechanism in the mind that is continuously working to avoid aloneness. It operates largely unconsciously and involuntarily and is sustained by this deep fear we seem to have of simply being with ourselves, and truly valuing the integrity of our aloneness. We are constantly seeking love from others; looking for recognition, confirmation, or a word of approval—and whenever we find them, we experience a sense of connection, which adds meaning to our lives. We are ruled by a powerful psychological need for belonging, from which we derive our sense of security—and this robs us of more of our freedom than we would like to admit.

Look at all the ways in which we tend to distract ourselves from simply being with ourselves: all the movies, the songs, our social activities and social contacts, watching TV, consuming comfort food, social media... If we would scrutinize our minds with sincerity and care, we will notice how with one sentence, a certain gesture, a facial expression, we somehow move out of ourselves, and try to hook up with the other. Whenever we do this, we forsake our aloneness, and in the same breath, lose a bit of our authenticity. We may notice how we tend to talk a lot, or how we try to sell ourselves in our conversations.

Even our spiritual disciplines—originally designed to get deeply in touch with ourselves—are sometimes executed in such a way that they undermine the very thing they were set up for. Practices like group meditation, group therapy, and the social comfort of a supporting spiritual community, can easily leave open a back door to escape the confrontational reality of simply being alone.

If we truly look at ourselves with complete honesty, many of us will find that we do just about anything to avoid simply being with ourselves. This is the psychology on which most of humanity operates. We keep cosying up to the consensus more than we know... How authentic is that really? Why are we so afraid to stand in our own truth? We seem to presume that others are a real source of love for us. But is this a trustworthy presumption to live from? Even if we *are* social creatures, how wise is it to live our lives as if our attachments to other people and objects are really the solution to the deep-rooted fear of our existential aloneness? Questioning ourselves like this, with healthy self-skepticism and sincerity, radically exposes all the ways in which we avoid our aloneness. It makes us realize that our continual avoidance does not bring about a deep, true, authentic way of living. Quite the contrary. It generates a mediocre quality of awareness, and a superficial quality of life.

If we want a life of more depth, we have to confront our fear of aloneness. We need to get to the heart of it, and crack its code, so that it can be seen through and dissolved. This is something we will never feel quite ready for. But that is exactly why *this* moment is as good as any to jump right in... Remember that the very thing we fear the most, is often our doorway to truth.

At first, entering into your aloneness may feel like falling into a big, black, desolate void, in which utter loneliness reigns. Your sense of being a separate self may intensify. So your first reflex will likely be to reach out again, and look for that sense of connectedness with others, in order to not feel your loneliness so bluntly. But reactivating that mechanism is an escape strategy—a quick-fix surrogate solution.

The best way to approach your loneliness is to simply stay present with it, without looking for a way out. Bear with it and allow it to be. The moment you can genuinely relax into your loneliness, its quality begins to change. Little by little, it begins to disintegrate. You move into a state in which everything simply feels okay the way it is. A clarity sets in—and in that clarity, all the unconscious strategies by which you tend to avoid your aloneness show themselves to you. Because you now see them for what they are, they will lose their power over you. They will no longer be able to pull you out of your depth so easily, and drag you into the superficial anxiety-awareness of sustaining attachments.

Then it becomes obvious to you that aloneness and loneliness are not synonymous, but rather each other's polar opposite. In loneliness, you feel not seen, unmet, cut off, separate, out of touch with yourself—as if all life is sucked out of you. But when you truly stand in your aloneness, you are most intimately in touch with yourself—and you feel utterly alive! The desolate black void you so feared reveals itself to be full—bubbling with aliveness and presence. Your fear of it evaporates, and aloneness becomes actually attractive. The more you are drawn into your aloneness, the more you can inhabit your own depth—which is the ground from which your authenticity blossoms. You begin to realize that no one else can truly understand what it means to be *you*. So, you will most naturally begin to live your life as your own unique journey—which no one can replicate.

So, genuine aloneness is a mature state of being in which the subtle undercurrent of anxiety that is sustained by your need to reach out and create attachments has come to rest. If you truly embody this quality of existence, the impact is far-reaching: The binding forces of your relative identity start to dwindle. You intuitively know that you are standing on the doorstep of the eternal, and one day, by grace, the door will open, and oneness will welcome you in. Then you will realize the secret promise of inhabiting your aloneness most radically. There *is* no other. There never has been. There is only one single reality, which is your very own being... And you will fill the entire universe with your presence!

Hans: *Beautiful...! Just to address the question on a more practical level as well... Does practicing aloneness mean that we have to literally seclude ourselves from our environment?*

136

Ameen: Not necessarily. Aloneness is a state of being first. It is not about becoming a hermit or denying life. On the contrary. In aloneness, you relate to life more intimately and freely, because you are rooted in a deeper state of presence and are no longer taken in tow so much by the anxiety of the mind.

Still, it is usually helpful for many people to actually take some time out once in a while. When you spend time in solitude, you eliminate at least the more obvious triggers of anxiety and restlessness, to which you are typically subjected in your interactions with daily life. You thereby undermine the activity of the mind's mechanisms of projecting, needing and searching—which makes it easier to fall into your own being-ness. That's why moments of deliberate solitude, or occasional retreats, can be very productive. Evidently, even the silence of a good retreat is no guarantee of a silent mind. But we know from all those who have done it, that secluding ourselves from our usual environment—even if only once in a while—is a proven pathway into deeper levels of silence.

Still, the bottom line about genuine aloneness is not so much about literal seclusion. Most essentially, aloneness is about a sustained moment-to-moment practice, right in the midst of life. You can observe the mechanisms of your mind right now. How am I reaching out right now? What am I attached to in this very moment? What takes me out of myself and undermines my sense of self-sufficiency? Piercing through the haze of automatic mental reactions, again and again, in many small moments every day, is the best way to surrender into your aloneness.

Perhaps curiously enough, the lessons of aloneness often become most clear right in the midst of life, and in relationship with others. Especially in romantic relationships, all the ways in which you avoid your aloneness tend to reveal themselves rather quickly, if you simply pay attention. When you are part of a couple, you may, for example, at times feel somewhat guilty about practicing aloneness, because it moves you out of the common dynamic of mutual confirmation. You may feel like you are abandoning the other, whereas—appropriately enough—you still want to be there for him or her. Your partner, in response, may

137

become somewhat anxious, because he or she feels you don't need them to feel fulfilled.

When you find the love that is within you—your own intimacy, your own wholeness your own well-being—you feel entirely self-sufficient. You have become your own best friend. You can enjoy going to a movie by yourself, munching on your popcorn, and reveling in the deep intimacy of your own company.

Such a sense of self-sufficiency obviously jeopardizes the unwritten contract inherent in relationships. It may cause discomfort in both partners because they know full well that a part of their relationship is centered around seeking consolation, creating attachment and avoiding aloneness—and that part is now eroding. They now face the challenge of integrating the new relational dynamic in one way or another—and the uncertainty this brings along may fuel a sense of insecurity.

Still, moving into a new relational dynamic doesn't necessarily mean what we all tend to fear: that the end of the relationship is near! There are skillful ways to navigate such a developmental shift. And if anything, aloneness is a sound basis for a healthier and stronger relationship. In genuine aloneness, your attention and awareness is liberated from the anxiety of the mind. All that attention and awareness is now freely available, and it can be invested in being much more fully present with your partner. So paradoxically, the moment you let go of the idea of 'other', you can be with the other most fully, because you are no longer distracted by your own agendas.

So, to learn the lessons of aloneness, you do not necessarily need to become a cave yogi. The lessons of life are too rich to be missed out on in seclusion. Embodying your aloneness right in the midst of life is the finest practice.

Hans: *The deepest possible silence is the silence of the awakened state. I am aware that the awakened state is said to be beyond words and is often described as indescribable. Still, it is also the goal of spiritual life, and our innermost reality as human beings. So it feels* *appropriate to try to hone in to it, in ways that brings it closer to home. I was wondering... could you talk about what it is like to live in the awakened state?*

Ameen: I could give it a try, but you already stated the challenge very accurately. Anything I might say is not the real thing. I can only talk about it in terms of certain qualities. But these qualities are not consciousness itself, for that is pure formless emptiness; a kind of living, awake presence that is unqualified—that is, most literally without any qualities. So to translate it into qualities is to limit it instantaneously, and, in fact, to miss the point.

At best, the qualities I could speak about are only ways in which consciousness *registers* in the body-mind. Some people use descriptions like: a vast transparent openness; a spaciousness that is timeless and formless. For others, it shows up mainly as a great clarity. For yet others, a sense of all-pervading oneness stands out. Some of the words I love to use are silence, freedom, presence and intimacy. But whatever words you favor, they are all merely reflections of what the awakened state actually is.

Still, if you can feel into the reality behind the language, it might actually convey a taste of the real thing. So with these qualifiers out of the way, I'll dive right in, and speak directly from that place...

It is totally clear to me that what I truly am is consciousness itself, without form, qualities or identity. Still, peripherally to that, I also know myself to be a body-mind with a personality. It's as if I am a nobody and a somebody at the same time. As a somebody, I engage in the world, and play the role my personality prompts me to play. But prior to that, I am always aware that my ultimate identity is like a vast clearing of silent presence, in which everything, including that role, is simply arising. Even as we are talking here, I experience both these realities simultaneously.

Ever since I 'woke up', the way I perceive the world around me has changed. When I look around, the objects I see are not just perceived as physical objects, but also seen as formless consciousness and energy.

139

When I look at the table over there, or at any object for that matter, I see the emptiness of it. In that sense, the entire creation doesn't seem solid—even though I know full well that, from an everyday point of view, it is definitely solid. If you throw a pebble against my head, you can be sure I'd experience that solidity. *(laughs)*

I evidently still experience our three-dimensional reality, and all of its properties, like anybody else. But there is an extra dimension added to my perception. It's as if the entire world is also breathing with consciousness. It is all vibrating. Even inanimate objects appear to be alive and radiant. They are all lit up, as if they have a soul.

I remember when I first saw a mountain again after awakening, I felt as if I could just walk right through it. During those early days, the contrast with how I perceived the world before was so stark that everything I set my eyes on struck me as magnificent. It all appeared utterly mysterious and stunningly beautiful—so much so, that it prompted a sense of deep ecstasy in me. Now, that initial feeling of wonder has subsided somewhat—as if I have grown used to this new way of perceiving. Still, what remains of it today is the sense that we are not living in a desolate universe full of dead matter.

This makes all the difference in the way you relate to your surroundings. It gives rise to an increased sense of appreciation, respect and care, which springs up most naturally when you realize that the same consciousness that is you is the very stuff everyone and everything else is made of. All of it is, at heart, one single reality.

One of my favourite words to allude to this all-pervading oneness is intimacy. To me, oneness is *quintessential* intimacy. I feel this quality of intimacy with everyone and everything, for no reason whatsoever. It is always present, even if the circumstances don't support it. It is my home base, whether I am in the heat of an argument; traveling in foreign countries, where nobody speaks my language; interacting with the cashier in the supermarket; or simply sitting alone in my room. I have always felt that the quality of intimacy quite accurately describes the felt sense of the awakened state.

In satsang, I use the word 'intimacy' more than I use abstract concepts like 'the absolute'. Intimacy is a feeling we can all relate to, in varying degrees. Before awakening, our sense of intimacy is still largely dependent on others' confirmation of our self-image or on the degree to which they share similar opinions and worldviews. But even this kind of conditional intimacy is beautiful. Feeling into its essence can give you a preliminary glimpse of the state of non-separation. It allows you to drop into your heart and aligns you with your innermost authentic self. It is a prelude to the unqualified intimacy of awakening: the radical oneness of consciousness itself.

When you wake up as that, it transforms your entire relationship to life. You then live in absolute intimacy with this very moment—with everything there is about it. You don't know of anything more precious. You simply understand how everything is born in this moment and dies in this moment. There is literally nothing but this moment. When you genuinely live in this understanding, you no longer take anything for granted. Even the most mundane things disclose themselves to be extraordinary: your own breathing, the sheer accuracy of the movement of your fingers, the workings of your senses, being able to communicate with others... You simply marvel at the mysterious wonder of it all. Whatever you set your eyes on, you see all of it as ornaments of the one single reality. All of it is at heart only consciousness, making love to itself. It sounds mystical; overly lyrical perhaps; but how else can I put the mystery of radical non-dual suchness into words? Perhaps I shouldn't... perhaps some things are better left untouched...

2

Discernment

Hans: *You make much of not giving away your authority and taking full responsibility for your own awakening process. Yet we all have our blind spots, and if we always only rely on ourselves, the dangers of self-deception are never far away. Can you speak about how to maintain the right balance between self-authority and accepting authority from sources other than ourselves? How do we navigate the tension between both in such a way that we prevent our evolution from running aground on some obstacle we might keep overlooking?*

Ameen: If you are committed to truth above all else, that very commitment itself has its ways of getting you back on track again and again. Nobody else can tell you with final authority what is true for you, or when you are fooling yourself.

However, it is a valid concern that such a powerful self-reliance may open the door for self-deception, because in real life, nobody's capacities for self-skepticism and sincerity are infallible. Even with the best of intentions, you may continue to overlook some of your obstacles or biases, and thereby keep sabotaging your own growth. A large part of what drives us is unconscious. We literally cannot see it. So it is always wise to stay open to input from sources other than yourself—like your friends, a psychologist, a spiritual teacher, a spiritual teaching, or wherever else the wisdom may come from—and where necessary, integrate it intelligently into your life.

But if you go so far as to make others your primary point of reference, you give away your power. This always ends up being counterproductive, because it diminishes the sense of responsibility you feel for your own awakening process—and thus it nibbles away at your whole-hearted involvement in it. This is my main concern about relying too heavily on external authorities. I have all too often seen how such reliance can stifle the aliveness of people's awakening process, and how it can deaden its thrust. So I always advise people to keep standing firmly on their own two feet. I found that an effective way to do so, is to learn to trust your own discriminative intelligence. In the end, the most powerful antidote against all forms of self-deception, including your shadows, is your living connection to your own discernment.

Yet this is often precisely where the shoe pinches... Some spiritual aspirants are hesitant to fully empower their faculty of discriminative intelligence, because its value is regularly downplayed in spiritual milieus—especially by schools that put more emphasis on surrender and devotion. Discriminative intelligence—so goes the argument—is about using the mind, and mind is the very thing you need to go beyond, if you truly want to wake up.

For all of its truth, a teaching like this doesn't seem to fully factor in that the mind is more than just a collection of compulsive patterns that needs to be outgrown. It is also the home of precious higher faculties. Discernment is one of them. It has nothing to do with the compulsive world of mental noise. Quite the contrary, in fact... Your discernment is really animated by your own deepest truth. This is why, far from being an impediment to the process of waking up, discernment is actually one of the finest means to help facilitate your awakening. Discernment will help you gain an accurate understanding of the workings of your mind. When it is fully empowered, it will eventually enable you to see right through the patterns of your mental apparatus. This is vital, because if you don't understand how your mind operates, you will be swept up in its habitual patterns all the time. But if you are able to see through them, they will loosen their grip on you, and you will drop into silence more easily.

The importance of cultivating an accurate understanding of the workings of the mind often comes up. Time and again people ask me: 'After satsang, I really felt in touch with a deep meditative silence. Then I went out into the world, and anxiety kicked back in. How can I best maintain a quality of silence in everyday life?' Employing your discriminative intelligence is the key to dealing with such matters. Inquire into why you lost your silence. At which point exactly did anxiety kick in again? What triggered it? Be aware of the subtleties involved. Were you reacting to someone's behavior, a certain glance, a type of body language?

If you keep inquiring into the patterns of your mind with sincere, intelligent, self-skeptical humility, in due course, your entire mental-egoic design will become obvious to you. You will see how it operates; how it creates identifications, attachments, separation from others, and how it causes suffering. Seeing all this with real clarity is the first step in freeing yourself from it. When the actual mechanism of your conditioning becomes conscious, it will no longer be able to exert its covert power over you. Its contracted, compulsive quality will begin to unwind. As a result, the noisy restlessness of your mind will quieten down, and a quality of open attentive awareness will take its place.

So there is an intimate relationship between using your discriminative intelligence and developing a silent mind. They mutually reinforce one another, and need to be cultivated together. Silence is where true intelligence is born, and true understanding catalyses a silent mind.

So I think that the most valuable response I can offer in answer to your question about the tension between not giving away your authority, while also remaining mindful of the pitfalls of self-deception, is to highlight the critical role of discriminative intelligence on the spiritual path.

Using your discriminative intelligence in honest self-inquiry allows you to expose your own game. It has the power to prevent you from being taken in tow by your own ambivalence. As long as your intention to wake up is sincere, you will *want* to ask yourself the hard questions—the ones that make you uncomfortable; the ones that will shake you up; the ones that force you to face parts of yourself you are deeply ashamed of—because you *know* that these are the ones that will set you free. You will simply not be interested in evading your obstacles, protecting your false personality, or escaping your shadows.

Intelligent self-inquiry, based on the sharpness of your own discernment, is the most potent way to pierce through your self-deception. It keeps you in touch with the inherent truthfulness of your deepest self. When you are plugged into that source, your own clarity will take over, and you will know when you are even slightly off track.

Using your discernment will also enable you to sense what you truly need to keep your process of waking up alive, and how to best invest your attention and energy.

You might be at a meditation retreat, and suddenly realize that what you really need is a dance party, because all that silent sitting is suffocating the creative flow of your life energy. You can simply sense that you will never drop into natural, unrepressed silence, as long as you are sitting on your energy... But you might also, under the same circumstances, realize that meditation is exactly what you need, right then and there, because your impulses to get up and do something else are caused by a compulsive restlessness you need to break free from—and you just know, that the right thing for you to do, to relax this condition, is to sit through many hours of silent meditation on retreat.

Your own discernment will show you your way. There are no ready-made manuals with general guidelines that account for all the intricacies of your own complexity; no external authorities that can tell you with finality what is true for you. In the end, your own discernment is your final authority. If you fully empower it, it will allow you to read yourself accurately. It will help you understand the needs of every part of yourself—you as body, mind, soul and spirit. All these dimensions of yourself require appropriate attention. If one or more of them are neglected, it compromises your overall growth. Embracing all these layers of your reality might be a tall order, but it is exactly what will allow you to fully inhabit your strength.

In the end, my work is about empowering students to take responsibility for their own awakening process; encourage them to investigate; and come up with their own answers. So what else can I tell you about self-authority but this: never give away your power. Inhabit the precious jewel of your discernment; and creatively craft your path as you go along—based on a living connection with your own sincerity. This is the pith of what my teaching stands for.

3

Shadow

Hans: *Our shadows powerfully determine the quality of our lives. They affect how we feel and shape the way we relate to others, particularly the tenacious ones that cause intense and recurrent emotional reactivity and hinder us from living a fulfilling life of clarity, sanity and freedom. So I think it's worth exploring the shadow in more depth. Could you start by explaining how shadows come into being, and how we can prevent new ones from being formed in us?*

Ameen: Shadows often come into being as a result of experiences or interactions with life we feel we cannot handle.

Perhaps some incident in your past triggered such intense emotions in you that you experienced them to be too overwhelming, so you closed down. It could have been anything imaginable. Perhaps your father used to be overly stern with you when you were young, and you crawled into your shell. Over time your withdrawal turned into an habitual pattern, and right up until today, even when there is no obvious trigger, you still feel uneasy in the company of men with an outspoken masculine presence... Perhaps you didn't know how to relate to some of your own instinctual impulses, vital energies, or bodily sensations, say, your own aggression, your sexuality, your sensuality. You experienced them to be confusing, disruptive, frightening... perhaps even downright

149

threatening. So rather than expressing them in healthy ways, you repressed them. You were afraid that they would come out wrong, or in socially unacceptable ways... Or perhaps you were ashamed of certain feelings you had; your own softness, your hardness, your bitterness... because you believed them to be undesirable. So you hid them away— even from yourself. The possibilities for shadow formation are almost infinite, and the shadow terrain itself is remarkably diverse.

The bottom line is that shadows are created whenever you run into some aspect of your own subjective experience that you cannot fully embrace as *really yours*. As a response, you push the unwanted quality out of your conscious awareness, as if it were *not really yours*. You banish it to your unconscious world—to that dusky subterranean zone in your psyche where all the shadows dwell. There, it continues to live in exile. You think you have gotten rid of it successfully—because you have made it unconscious. But in fact, you have only split off an actual piece of your own inner experience, and moved it to your unconscious zone.

So, in reality, that unwanted quality is still very much a part of you, and as such, it can still be stirred up. Whenever that occurs, it comes out as some form of emotional reactivity; a sudden emotional charge that feels disturbing to you and catches you by surprise. As long as these unwanted qualities are not yet fully embraced, they will spring up from your unconscious zone whenever they are triggered—and they will continue to trouble you, pull your strings and run your life.

It never ceases to amaze me how creative our psyche really is in coming up with ways to make our unwanted subjective qualities unconscious. We repress, reject, withdraw, dissociate, rationalize, deny and project—just to name a few. Psychology calls these interior maneuvers 'defense mechanisms', and the understanding is that whenever any of these mechanisms is activated, shadow material is being built up or maintained.

Now, if the inability to accommodate unwanted qualities in our awareness is the origin of shadow formation, then one of the ways to prevent new shadows from being born is to strengthen our capacity to stay present with these qualities when they arise. In other words: to learn to hold them in our awareness without activating our defense mechanisms. Developing this capability can be challenging, because these defense mechanisms are largely unconscious, involuntary, and deeply ingrained in our psyche. They have usually already self-activated well before we are aware of them.

Thus, simply staying open and present, without activating any of these forms of avoidance, is a true life art. It requires us to step into each new moment as fresh, alive and full of creative potential, rather than to simply go along with the deadened habitual patterns our psyche usually operates on. This doesn't just happen by itself. It calls for moment-by-moment practice:

First, you need to become aware of all the little ways in which you tend to cringe, go numb, or turn away from aspects of your own subjective experience.

Then, when you do feel yourself turn away from something, just choose to remain intimately involved with it instead—even when you feel it to be overwhelming, undesirable, threatening, shameful, painful, negative, frightening, confusing, and so on. Be willing to open yourself up, again and again, in every new moment, no matter what arises. The moment you allow yourself to turn away from any inner feeling, you prepare and fertilise the breeding ground for shadow.

If all these subjective qualities are allowed to arise in you, as they will, and you remain open and present, none of them will turn into shadows, and resurface in unhealthy ways. None of them will become perverted, or get twisted into neuroses and cause harm to yourself or others.

If you practice this inner gesture of open presence, and you do it with focused sincerity, you will remain intimately connected to the totality of your own experience. And that, to me, is sanity.

151

Hans: *If shadows are parts of ourselves that we keep unconscious, how then can we spot them in ourselves?*

Ameen: Right... It is true that our shadow material is no longer *directly* in our view because it is unconscious. But unconscious doesn't mean untraceable. You can still discover it in indirect ways. One of the markers of shadow that is almost infallible is emotional reactivity. Whenever you feel reactivity arise in you, however subtle, you can almost be ceratian that a shadow knot has been triggered. Usually this happens quickly and unexpectedly. It catches you off guard. Something happens, or somebody says something to you, and suddenly you are no longer fully in the present moment. You are sucked into identification with some residue from the past; some psychological pattern you don't have much control over.

Perhaps you feel disturbed, but you just can't lay your finger exactly on what causes this disturbance. So you know that in order to find out, you need to dive a bit deeper into your psyche, and keep questioning yourself, until you are clear about your answer... Maybe you overreacted to something that had been said to you. Even if what was said was truly not the most sensitive thing you ever heard, why did *you* react disproportionately, whereas someone else might have just let it pass by? What are the specific emotional mechanics in your case? Your answers to such questions are road signs into your shadow zone... Maybe someone pointed something out to you about your behavior, and you refuse to self-reflect on it, because you are convinced you are right. Why are you so sure? Are you right? Do they have no point at all? Maybe they don't, but... chances are they do. Still, you can't see this inconvenient truth about yourself, because you are so closely identified with your conviction that you consider it to be totally justified... Whatever the case may be, the point is that emotional reactivity most often suggests the presence of a shadow issue.

Still, shadow is not all about negative emotions only. Even a positive emotional charge could point to the presence of shadow. Perhaps you are tremendously enthusiastic about some wonderful characteristic in someone. You may, for example, find yourself admiring and praising someone's rhetorical skills all the time. Most likely, this person is a brilliant rhetorician indeed. Still, the whole truth might be that being skillful with words is, in fact, your own disowned strength that you, for some reason, don't dare to pursue, and that you therefore now abundantly project onto others.

So whenever any kind of emotional reactivity arises in us, positive or negative, and we find ourselves losing our presence, being thrown off balance, or being pushed out of our center somehow, that's a sign that a shadow has been touched in us. Thus, our emotional temperature is definitely something to watch closely, if we want to become more conscious about our shadows.

That being said, it remains important to keep articulating that emotional reactivity is not the shadow itself. It is just the tip of the iceberg. Deep below the water surface, the actual iceberg floats, hidden from our view—just like our shadows. Discovering these shadows requires a deep dive into our psyche—and this is what we call shadow work.

This kind of work, however, invariably begins by exploring our emotional reactivity. The reason is clear enough: unlike our shadows, our emotional reactivity is conscious, and in our view. It is therefore the most reliable lead we have into the unknown territory of our shadow zone.

So by exploring our reactivity, and being attentive to all the clues it contains, we will eventually be able to trace it back to its source, and bring to light the shadow that is causing it.

Working with our shadows like this can be pretty straightforward. But it can also turn out to be a bit of a puzzle. It all depends on how deep-seated our shadows really are, and on how distorted the actual connection between the reactivity and the shadow has become.

Sometimes, the link is easy enough to grasp. If you routinely get terribly upset, for example, whenever you encounter stubbornness in

153

others, then chances are that you have a problem facing up to your own stubbornness, and have therefore turned it into a shadow. Because you can't handle it in yourself, you now project it all around you. You see it in everybody else, except in yourself.

So in cases like this, the reactivity and the shadow are both about the same emotional quality—that is: stubbornness. Shadows like that are not too much of a riddle. You just need to work on acknowledging them in yourself.

In other cases, it may be just a matter of being more honest with yourself. Stop telling yourself stories that are not factually true. Some people have persistent stories running through their minds about what incorrigible losers they are, or... about what amazing winners they are, and how everything they touch turns into gold. Their storylines have turned into a mental pattern that is disconnected from reality. In cases like these, you simply have to correct your inner narrative, and replace it with a more realistic self-interpretation. The problem here is quite obvious. You don't need to figure out that much.

But sometimes, the connection between your reactivity and your actual shadow is not that straightforward at all. Your shadow may even re-surface as a different emotional quality. If that is the case, shadow work requires a bit more discernment.

Perhaps you feel sad or depressed, yet the real unconscious cause of these symptoms is your repressed anger. Because anger is utterly unacceptable to you, you have repressed it so intensely that you don't feel it anymore as the raw, direct emotion that it is. Instead, you feel it indirectly, as a different emotional quality. It now shows up in your awareness as sadness and depression.

So in this particular case your first task is to take ownership of your anger—the real shadow. Working with its symptoms of sadness and depression will be fruitless. Only when you address your actual shadow head-on, and transform it, its symptoms of sadness and depression will disappear as well.

154

Emotions can shift into other emotions, after your defense mechanisms have done their job on them, and this is what can make shadow work feel like groping in the dark. It is also why you cannot simply take a quick look inside, and start working with what appears in your awareness. You need to take your inquiry further—all the way down into your unconscious zone—and deal with the actual source of your emotional reactivity. Chiseling away at the tip of the iceberg won't suffice. You have to take the plunge, deep below the waters surface, and deal with the ice mass from beneath.

So our shadows are often not what they appear to be. Sometimes, they are entirely invisible to us. That means that self-deception is always a real possibility. Therefore it is surely wise to seek the professional guidance of a therapist, or at least work with someone else who knows you, has open eyes, and can reflect back to you. Your close relationships are often your clearest mirrors.

Still, the driving force behind your shadow work should always be your own sincerity. Your own sincere engagement is your most powerful weapon for cutting through self-deception. Just remember that there is a great deal about yourself that you don't yet know. But as long as sincerity is awake in you, you will always remain inquisitive about the unknown corners of your emotional world. You will remain curious about why you react the way you do, rather than ensconce yourself in what you already know about yourself. If you keep exploring your inner world with real curiosity, and a healthy dose of self-skeptical humility, slowly but surely, you will begin to see through your reactivity, and meet your shadows hidden underneath.

Hans: *That's a helpful clarification about the way shadow material is structured in our psyche. But how do we work with this understanding in our everyday lives? Let's say that I have identified some concrete emotional issue that bothers me, because it keeps resurfacing. How can I actually work with that, in such a way that my shadow* *will effectively dissolve?*

Ameen: I should probably start by saying that the success of shadow work depends on how willing you really are to face your own demons. Not everybody is keen to do this. Remember that shadows are the product of feelings, emotions or sensations you are ashamed of, threatened by, overwhelmed by, and so on. So your natural tendency is to turn away from them. But shadow work requires you to do the exact opposite. It is really meant to help you turn *towards* your disowned emotions; look them squarely in the eye; and re-identify with them. The way you do this is by progressively imbuing them with presence. Permeate them with awareness, until they no longer appear as unconscious reactivity, but as conscious emotions—clear, open and sane.

So, whenever you feel emotional reactivity well up in you, don't just go along with it, until you lose yourself in it. Treat it more consciously.

First, feel into your emotional charge, without turning away. Simply stay present with it. Allow it to be. Don't judge it. Don't repress it. Don't deny it. Don't justify it. Don't add any reaction to it. Just let it show up exactly the way it does. Then feel into its textures. Which qualities does it contain? Familiarize yourself with them. Can you feel where the emotional pressure is located in your body? Hone into this spot as precisely as you can. Feel it out... Bringing more awareness to your reactivity starts by establishing a feeling-relationship with it, without giving in to the natural tendency to turn away.

Then, go deeper. Examine your emotional reactivity up close. Question it with discernment and real curiosity. What is the story around this particular emotional pattern? In which situations does it usually arise? Why do I continue to hold on to it? Am I afraid of losing something? What do I tend to deny, and why? Why do I consistently dramatize this particular feeling? Ask precisely those questions that you intuitively sense will guide you straight to the core of your issue.

Then be quiet. Hold these questions in your awareness, and listen to what your emotions are truly telling you. What message does their very existence convey to you? Know that your emotions contain information about your own truth.

Your anger, for example, might tell you that a boundary you hold dear has been crossed. But to the degree that your anger has turned into a reactive pattern, it contains an inauthentic component as well. Your job is to discriminate between the authenticity and the inauthenticity in your anger. What is the real function of this emotion for you? What is the legitimate need contained within it? And where did it become distorted? Sort that out...

By inquiring like this you will come to understand the real marrow of your disowned emotion, its raison d'être—the shadow quality hidden at its core. This is a significant step. It means you have now seen through an aspect of yourself that was previously still unconscious. And such an understanding will further permeate your shadow world with more awareness.

When you have thus understood your actual shadow, it is time to make the completing move of the shadow process: to re-identify with your disowned emotion, and make it part of your conscious awareness again.

To do this, feel it as really yours, even if it still feels shameful, weird or uncomfortable. Allow its raw energy in your awareness, without giving in to the tendency to avoid it once again. Simply trust that you won't merely be reduced to it. Embrace it wholeheartedly. Allow it to arise in you as it will. You cannot successfully eliminate it anyway. Any attempt to do so would drive it into the shadows again. So, accept it fully and embody it with your whole being. In short: *be it!*

It sometimes helps to keep in mind that any emotion we tend to turn away from is simply part of human nature. Every conceivable emotion lives in us. Whether it is anger, fear, jealousy, grief, sadness, envy, pride or anything else, all such emotions are simply products of our separate sense of self. We all carry around pockets of emotions we find undesirable in ourselves, and all of us have hidden corners in our psyche where we might feel flawed, unlovable, unsuccessful, insufficient, uninteresting, superficial, dull or boring—emotions we feel ashamed or uncomfortable about. So, we devise strategies to avoid feeling them, and we want to hide them from others. That is how shadow got created in the first place. But even the truths we don't want to recognize about ourselves are an intrinsic part of who we are. Nothing to be ashamed about. Nothing to be afraid of. So it is only authentic to embrace those truths too.

The moment you are able to do this, there is a profound change within. The quality of awareness becomes clearer, more conscious and more open. You are now able to stay fully present with your emotions—without turning away. So whenever they arise, they can circulate through you freely, exactly as they are, without being distorted by your defense mechanisms. When this is the case, you have effectively re-owned your shadows. They now no longer appear as emotional reactivity—and as such, they carry an entirely different flavor.

Let's look at aggression, for example. In its repressed mode, it expresses itself as a neurosis, and it tends to show up as a force of attack or destruction. Because it is unconscious, you cannot work with it directly and you cannot master it. It tends to erupt in random and blind ways, but aggression as a neurosis is not authentic aggression. Its source is frustration, disturbance—not the passion to move things forward. In its re-owned expression, aggression is simply a healthy force that cuts through obstacles and gets things done. It is powerful, life-giving, catalyzing energy that doesn't find its source in mere reactivity. In its healthy version, aggression is owned like a tool. It allows you to speak to a thousand people with passion. But it can only manifest this way if it is not distorted by the workings of inner defense mechanisms, if you are firmly rooted in your center, and if you come from a place of sincerity.

So you see, working on your shadows to the point of re-owning them can be profoundly liberating. It can make your life so much richer, less rigid, less one dimensional, and much more free. When you re-own your shadows, you will show up as more authentic, more open, more vibrant and more natural—others will feel this in your energy. Haven't you noticed that people with little shadow material are more in touch with the richness of life, and with their own humanity? They do not contract so easily in the face of difficulty. They are more transparent. You can sense that they have lost their hidden agendas—so you feel they are more trustworthy. They have worked through a wide range of human emotions, and you can feel their familiarity with whatever you bring to them. Nothing seems alien to them, and not much can shock them. So in their presence, you too tend to feel more comfortable and at ease.

Hans: *That sounds as if there is an enormous potential locked up in our shadow that is just waiting to be set free...*

Ameen: That's exactly right. It is astounding how much energy and awareness is locked up in our shadows. Keeping our shadows intact takes a certain effort—albeit an unconscious one, and keeping our defense mechanisms up and running consumes a lot of our energy. This means that whenever you repress or deny some aspect of yourself— whether it is sensuality, emotional-sexual energy, feelings, or unwanted thoughts and impulses—some of your energy and awareness contracts around that particular aspect. It gets trapped there and can thus no longer circulate freely through your system. This can create all sorts of repercussions. Perhaps you experience a diminishment of the vibrancy of your life force; perhaps you notice a clouding in the clarity of your awareness; perhaps you feel out of touch with certain feelings, vital energies, emotions or impulses; or perhaps you simply do not notice any effects at all, because you have grown so used to your condition that you have a hard time imagining yourself in a different state... In whatever way the particulars may manifest, the bottom line is that your shadow directly impacts the quality of your awareness and affects the way you show up in your life.

Most often you only realize the extent of this impact when you manage to liberate yourself from some shadow. Suddenly, you feel released in very profound ways, as liberated energy and awareness fill the space where your shadow used to be. You feel re-energized, more open, more free—and this will not go by unnoticed. It will be written all over your face; it will be visible in the authenticity of your smile; it will translate in the naturalness of your body language; and it will inevitably show up in your behavior and actions.

But as long as we keep ignoring shadow work, all this wonderful potential will remain out of reach—neatly locked up in our shadow zone. The consequences of ignoring shadow work can be quite impactful—so much so, that in some cases, it could even bring someone's inner development to a halt.

Inner development, such as psychological growth or spiritual awakening, requires a certain momentum of energy and awareness in order to keep moving into further levels of maturity. Sometimes, there might simply not be enough momentum to catalyze further growth, because too much energy and awareness are bound up in our shadows—and so our development stagnates. This is unfortunate, since with the right kind of attention, this situation can be remedied. Focused shadow work has the power to liberate this trapped energy and awareness and make it available again for further growth. The moment it is freed up, it will naturally reinvest itself in those areas where our developmental process needs it most. It's a mysterious dynamic—and it seems to follow its own intelligent logic.

In my work I can sometimes see this dynamic in action: some people tell me that they feel stuck in their meditative practice. They just can't get their minds quiet. Whenever they sit down to meditate, all they experience is anxiety and restlessness. The cause is often a psychological pattern that keeps flaring up, or an emotional atmosphere they just can't seem to shake off. Very often, the dissolution of the shadow knot that corresponds to that persistent pattern, or the unwinding of some pocket of repressed energy, is exactly what they need to break through the deadlock and move into a deeper level of silence. In cases like this, the dissolution of shadow material clearly benefits the process of spiritual awakening.

So if you intend to keep your inner growth alive, and live in freedom, clarity and sanity, sincere shadow work will always be one of your greatest allies. It frees up energy and awareness which provide the juice for genuine breakthroughs into further potentials of yourself—potentials you might have intuited all along, but perhaps never thought of as actually within your reach. And thus, it often happens that sincere shadow work leads you right into a long awaited new chapter in your life.

Hans: *Despite the benefits of shadow work, many people have become skeptical or discouraged about doing it. Some have grown convinced that they cannot really change in any meaningful way. Others have grown weary of shadow work because it feels like an endless endeavor. They don't want to keep digging up all the details of their personal history, and they definitely don't want to spend half of their lives on the therapist's couch, talking about their dads. They point out that you can be working on your negative emotions for decades, without truly transforming them in any lasting manner. How realistic are the prospects for genuine transformation?*

Ameen: I understand these concerns—and if we look at conventional therapy, we all too often see them turn into reality. More often than not, the end result of therapy is that you have simply learned some new way to deal with your issues when they arise. You might have learned to channel your emotions in a socially acceptable way; or activate a different attitude towards them; or translate them into a more desirable behavioral response. Whatever the case may be, conventional therapy is not likely to help you dissolve your issues in any lasting way. A therapist often cannot do much more than validate and reassure you—if he doesn't want to risk triggering your defense mechanisms even more —as he helps you recognize some pain or anger. For an all too great a number of people, therapy does not surpass the level of a comfort procedure.

Still, the belief that human beings might be unable to change in any fundamental way is not one that I like to encourage. You are always going to hear from me that, in a spirit of earnest practice, genuine transformation *can* occur. The sincerity of your willingness to face your shadows and the strength of your intention to do so are the keys.

But you always have to keep in mind that shadow work has a very particular purpose; and rather than get discouraged about doing it, it is more fruitful to remain aware of what it is intended to do. It is not about turning you into a saint, by making your negative emotions disappear once and for all. Rather, it is meant to help you take full ownership of them when they arise. Shadow work will prepare you to stay fully present with your negative emotions. You will no longer tend to push them out of your awareness because you feel overwhelmed by them or consider them to be undesirable. The effect of shadow work will be that your emotions no longer appear as unconscious reactive symptoms of some covert emotional reality. Instead, they will now show up as straightforward, raw expressions of the authentic 'you'—fully owned, fully conscious, and no longer distorted by the workings of your defense mechanisms. Thus, shadow work brings back authenticity to your emotional world.

Re-owning your shadows is valuable progress. It means that whenever some negative emotion bubbles up, you can more freely choose to express yourself differently. Since you are now fully aware of it, you also have a grip on it. Its compulsive character is gone, and thus you can more easily take responsibility for it.

So even though your negative emotions will likely still be there after shadow work, the fact that they are now re-owned, out in the open, and no longer unconscious, gives them an entirely different flavor. And this is what the shadow work process, as I described it earlier, *can* deliver.

But if you want to take it further, and actually transform your negative emotions so profoundly that their negative character is purged, a purely psychological approach will not suffice. If shadow work is to have such thorough results, it needs to be enacted in an overarching spiritual context. The reason is straightforward: without a well-developed awareness of who you are *beyond* the mind, it is hard to untie knots *within* the mind. As long as you feel exclusively and thoroughly identified with your mental-emotional patterns—as long as you are convinced that they are who you are—it is hard to let go of them. A spiritual approach has the power to loosen up the grasping forces that keep this narrow sense of identity intact. Spiritual practices, like meditation, are designed to help you widen your sense of identity and shift it to your witnessing awareness beyond the mind. From there, whatever contents come up within the mind can be looked at much more easily, worked with and released—because you will no longer feel them to be your core identity. If the contents of your mind are not really who you are, why would you still defend them so fiercely? Why would you still find it so hard to let go of them? Instead, you will very likely remain open and curious whenever some emotional charge wells up in you, or when somebody confronts you with your shadows. The pure awareness of the witness is non-resistant and wide. It provides the necessary space in which your entire psychological world can be freely embraced, relaxed, and eventually released.

The secret of genuine transformation of negative emotions lies in the boundless transparency of witnessing awareness. The more you can hold your negative emotions in the spaciousness of pure awareness, the more they will be cleansed of their unfavorable features and the more they will be liberated from their contracted density. Then, one day, you will simply notice that all their narrowness has been washed away... utterly released in the limitless expanse of consciousness itself. Without this space of release the witnessing awareness offers, it is hard to dissolve negative emotions with any kind of finality.

163

This is why the psychological process needs to be completed with a spiritual process. Both psychology and spirituality play their own unique and irreplaceable roles in the transformation of emotions. The psychological dimension of shadow work is a necessary first step. You need to become aware of your shadows first. You cannot bring witnessing presence to that which is still unconscious in you. So, before you can effectively release your negative emotions, you have to re-own them. Then, the spiritual process can begin to work its wonders, and gently crystallize your negative emotions, until only their pure essence remains.

4

Crystallizing Emotions

Hans: *You have spoken at length about the psychological process of re-owning emotions, and briefly touched on the spiritual process of crystallizing them until only their essence remains. Can you clarify this spiritual way of working with emotions a bit further?*

Ameen: Sure. As I explained before, re-owning emotions makes them authentic again—straightforward, and undistorted by the workings of your defense mechanisms. But even authentic emotions are still expressions of your separate self-sense. You are still thoroughly identified with them. Therefore, even your most authentic emotions are still ego-bound—and still somewhat narrow and self-absorbed. They are no longer so tightly contracted that you push them out of your awareness and into the shadows, but they are still enclosed within a sphere of contracted energy.

The spiritual way of working with emotions is about relaxing this sphere of self-contraction, in which your emotions are embedded, and thereby liberating them from their quality of self-involvement and self-concern. As this occurs, something truly remarkable happens. Your emotions begin to take on an entirely different flavor. They are transmuted into their pure essence! This is the little known secret of our emotional reality... All your emotions—even the negative ones—

carry some precious quality at their core—some intrinsic wisdom that is usually not obvious at first glance. They all harbor an original intelligence, a unique beauty, a beneficial quality that cannot fully play its role, unless it is released. When you engage with your emotions from a foundation of sincere spirituality, and liberate them from the forces of egoic grasping, eventually, their pure essence will be released.

If you feel into your anger, for example, you might begin to get a real sense of its intrinsic wisdom. As you attune to its core, chances are that you will begin to notice a great clarity; a penetrating intelligence; a clear-seeing wisdom. Right at the heart of your anger, you may find a clarity so powerful that it fills you with juice, passion, intensity and enormous strength. When your anger is expressed as these non-contracted qualities at its core, it feels entirely different than when it is expressed in its everyday, narrow, and at times vicious form. In its crystallized form, your anger may be used as a corrective force that clears out confusion and restores the integrity of a situation gone wrong. Crystallized anger is sheer power and unsullied clarity—and because of its uncontracted, trans-egoic quality, it can be put in service of a greater good.

The spiritual process of crystallizing emotions is deeply transformative. Supporting or quickening it can therefore be profoundly fulfilling. You can do so by holding your emotions with witnessing presence:

Whenever some powerful emotion arises, turn to that which is aware of it. Anchor yourself in that mysterious feeling of being that is already completely awake, alive and conscious in you—no matter what arises. Simply stay clear and present during the rise and fall of the natural cycle of the emotion. Your own pure awareness is your place of rest and reference prior to it. Notice that the transparency of pure awareness is never colored by your emotions. It is ever pristine—untouched by anything that is appearing within it. Do you notice its freedom, its spaciousness, its imperturbable silence? To you as the witness, your emotions are simply objects circulating through your awareness—nothing more.

They come and they go. They are not what you are. As you anchor yourself in the witness, your sense of self widens. You now spontaneously dis-identify from your emotion... Now notice the surprising effect. As the atmosphere of self-contraction in which the emotion is embedded relaxes, a fresh energy emerges—one that had been there all along, but that you had heretofore not noticed. The essential flavor of the emotion is gently liberated, and begins to shine forth.

Engaging with your emotions in this way will keep the process of crystallizing them alive in you. And when the time is ripe, they will turn into their awakened expression.

Looking back, I can now see the many ways in which this crystallization process has been at work in my own life.

As a child, for example, I was shy and introverted. Yet somehow I intuited, from early on, that there was also a precious quality hidden deep inside that painful shadow. It harbored an essence of intimate quietude, which I sensed to be a part of my true character. In those early days, however, most of my quietness came out of my shyness. Shyness is based on fear. There is a contraction in it—and wherever there is a contraction, you are not in your natural state. Real quietude is not based on fear at all. It comes from an already silent mind. Nowadays my shyness has gone, but I still have a quiet nature. My quietude is no longer supported by a shadow, like it used to be. It is full of conscious presence. There is no avoidance in it. It has morphed into its awakened expression.

For me, the crystallization of shyness into quietude was a deep and slow process. It started somewhat hesitantly when I was still a child, and only came to full fruition after awakening, when my egoic identification with this negative emotion was undone, and its true essence could begin to emerge.

My silent nature is now a support in my role as a spiritual teacher. It generates a meditative atmosphere. My silence somehow catches on with others and renders them silent too.

The crystallization of emotional qualities is a generous event. It brings about your most authentic self-expression in life. It unleashes the real depth, the richness, and the sanity of your emotional world. Crystallized emotions are powerful. They are free-flowing, uncontracted energy—and since they are by nature more mature, and less self-involved, they will be more embracing. And so they will more liberally be put in service of others. As such, the crystallization of your emotions is the capstone of the shadow process.

Hans: *The presence of shadow after awakening is a prominent theme in your life story. However, the understanding that shadow can still play a distorting role after awakening doesn't seem to be the uncontested general consensus in the spiritual world. In fact, I have heard spiritual teachers claim that they are beyond shadow plain and simple. Can you explain why it is possible at all that there can still be shadow residue left after awakening? Why doesn't the shadow wake up too? Isn't the realization that you are only consciousness by definition the kiss of death for your identification with your ego and its shadows?*

Ameen: When spiritual teachers defend the idea that the state of one's shadow constellation is not really relevant for the quality of awakened awareness, they often maintain that, by its very nature, consciousness itself always remains pure, empty and untouched—no matter what arises within it. It is the prior condition in which all experiential contents appear—including shadows. Being formless, consciousness is never reduced to any of these contents, nor is it ever tainted by them. Therefore—so goes the argument—shadow is simply not relevant if awakening as consciousness is authentic. This line of reasoning is quite common in spiritual milieus, especially in so-called Neo-Advaita circles.

When I first heard about it, right after awakening, it caused considerable confusion in me—even to the point of doubting my own awakening. On the one hand, I could see the truth of this claim in my own experience. Whenever shadow reactivity came up in me, it felt utterly inconsequential, negligible, and irrelevant—for I had seen that what I truly was, was this field of consciousness that is inherently uncontaminated by whatever appears within it. I could quite easily relate to the assertion that shadow is not relevant if awakening is authentic. From the point of view of consciousness itself, it made perfect sense.

But if I was genuinely sincere with myself, I also had to admit that, whenever shadow reactivity did arise, it still compromised the clarity of my awareness. During such moments, it felt as if my sense of oneness had been diminished, and my intimacy with life had been reduced. The fact that, even after awakening, shadow seemed to keep interfering with my deepest aspiration—to be fully intimate with life—bothered me beyond compare. I wanted my awareness to retain that sense of transparency, intimacy and expansion that is intrinsic to it, all the time.

I felt stuck in a strange paradox—and both sides of it were true. I couldn't wrap my head around it... If my identity was truly consciousness itself—pristine and untouched—then why did it seem to be affected the moment shadow reactivity resurfaced? Why had awakening not erased my shadows? How could both shadow and awakening be present simultaneously?

As I struggled with these questions, I began to grasp that, even after awakening, the most basic ways in which the self is organized don't change all that much. The self still contains areas that are conscious, and other areas that are still unconscious—such as your shadows. What *does* change with awakening is that the self-contraction in the conscious areas of the self drops away, as your narrow, egoic identity is replaced by the open clearing of consciousness itself. But the unconscious areas of the self remain essentially unaffected. Awakening cannot really touch that which is still unconscious in you—and so it doesn't transform your shadows. Before your shadow material can effectively 'wake up' too, so to speak, it needs to be re-integrated into your conscious awareness first. So, as I kept scanning myself for answers, I came to understand that even though awakening erases the self-contraction from the conscious areas of the self, it still leaves *pockets of self-contraction* intact here and there. These unconscious knots remain essentially sealed off from the liberating impact of awakening.

Now, when you remain secluded from life, or sit in silent meditation, absorbed in the mystery of awakened awareness, as I tended to do, there is a good chance that these pockets of self-contraction will remain dormant, and cause no shadow reactivity. There are no disruptions in formless emptiness. Still, they are floating in your inner space somewhere—and when you begin to engage in life again, sooner or later, they will be triggered, and you will no longer be able to deny them. Suddenly you will notice that your absorption in consciousness is not as deep as it could be. You will realize that you have been sucked into some emotional residue from your past and have lost a bit of your conscious presence in the now. You have forgotten your own true nature for a moment—and you will have to admit to yourself that your clarity, transparency and freedom are being compromised because of this. It's not unlike a marathon runner who suddenly notices a little stone in his shoe. He can still run the entire marathon, but his run won't be as smooth.

So, as I grappled with my post-awakening challenges, it became increasingly clearer to me that, even though it is true that consciousness itself can never be threatened, your *abiding as* consciousness itself *can* be threatened. It *can* be compromised by the contents of consciousness—especially by those that carry a powerful emotional charge, coming from your unconscious mind, like your shadows. Awakening will not magically undo these unconscious knots. You still remain secretly connected to them—and from their hiding place in your unconscious zone, they will continue to exert an undefined magnetic pull over you. So every now and then, they will still throw you off balance.

And so it dawned on me, during these wonderful, but puzzling, early post-awakening years, that awakening and shadow *can* and *do* coexist. Awakening is not the all-or-nothing event it is sometimes proclaimed to be.

Eventually I came to understand how this view, that shadow is not relevant if awakening is authentic, is often supported by a very radical interpretation of the relationship between the absolute and the relative reality—an interpretation in which the absolute is overemphasized. This radical view asserts that consciousness alone is real, whereas the individual self with its shadows is nothing but a mere illusion—and therefore not worth paying much attention to. It is not necessary to improve it; not necessary to clean up its shadows. It simply needs to be recognized for the mirage it really is.

But such a view fails to acknowledge that, due to the actual non-dual oneness of relative and absolute, both consciousness as such *and* the individual self with its shadows are in some profound way equally important. After all, the relative self is the instrument through which pure consciousness expresses itself—and thus it is paramount to have your instrument as fine-tuned as it can be. If you overlook this crucial point, you will tend to invalidate the need for continued shadow work—and this can quickly turn into a serious problem.

This is a big part of why we went through this culture-wide puzzlement over the seemingly unstoppable stream of controversial behavior by so many spiritual teachers. Their shadow knots hadn't been cleaned up. These knots were still an *actual part* of their personality structure, and therefore, they were bound to be expressed in their lives in one way or another. There is no way around that. The entirety of your personality complex will simply be used by you—as the true self—to interact with life.

So, waking up as consciousness itself—however impactful—is not the end game. Most people need to move through an elaborate post-awakening process that is centred around integrating their realization of consciousness as such with their body-mind. Their instrument needs to be attuned to the new reality of awakened awareness. If this process is impeded in any way or discounted, they will find themselves trying to express pure consciousness through a faulty vehicle—and this leads to a less than awakened self-expression. It gives rise to the uncomfortable paradox we so often have to deal with in relationship with our spiritual teachers: We enjoy their beneficial awakening power and brilliant dharma transmissions, while at the same time being impacted unfavorably in certain areas of our lives, because leftover shadow materials still taint the teacher's expression here and there—often unknowingly.

In light of this, many have wondered whether working with a teacher is worth it. I still think it is—even if it hasn't been my own path. Awakening is such little-known territory that, for most people, a relationship with a teacher proves to be greatly beneficial. A qualified teacher can offer valuable guidance and direct transmission of awakened awareness. The caveat is that both the teacher and the student alike need to assume a healthy responsibility for their roles.

From the student's side, working with a teacher requires seriousness and receptivity, but also discernment, open eyes and a certain maturity. It's about maintaining a healthy balance between what you absorb, and what you reject, because the last thing you want to receive from your awakened teacher is a quality of his shadow residue.

The teacher, from his side, needs to possess a proper understanding of the workings of the shadow, demonstrate a sincere commitment to keep working on his issues, and be transparent about his weaker sides.

This kind of vulnerable honesty would give rise to a different relational style between teacher and student than the one we have all heard stories about—and it looks like that's where we are heading. The newly emerging teacher-student model has relinquished the myth of the perfect guru and the absolute authority that often flows forth from that notion—and it is based on the understanding that one hundred percent purity can never be reached. As a teacher, relating to your students in such a spirit requires a different kind of courage—one that has its own challenges. But it will, at least in my opinion, create a spiritual culture of greater transparency, mutuality and accountability.

For a long time, this whole matter of the nature of the shadow, and the significance of shadow work, was not really understood very well in spiritual circles. Awakening was all too often portrayed as the end of evolution, and this interpretation tends to render any kind of further post-awakening maturation irrelevant. Only recently did this begin to shift. And I believe it will change the spiritual world for the better. Together with the precious gift of awakened awareness, it will also bring about greater psychological maturity. And investing the right kind of attention in both these areas of our human potential will move us all closer to a deeper fulfillment of the bright promise of a genuine non-dual realization: living a freedom that is both beyond life, and radically in the midst of it.

Hans: *If enlightenment is not the end of evolution, as you just suggested, is it at all possible then to be fully enlightened?*

Ameen: To me, the idea of 'final enlightenment' doesn't make much sense. That's why I prefer to use the word 'awakening' instead. Throughout the ages the notion of 'enlightenment' has become infused with an aura of finality and perfection—and I don't want to keep affirming that connotation.

That doesn't mean I am using the word 'awakening' lightly—as if it were merely some momentary insight, or even a more prolonged experience of some elevated spiritual state. To me 'awakening' still refers to the recognition of your own true nature as consciousness itself: formless, changeless and unqualified. This recognition usually occurs in a particular *moment of awakening*. There is indeed a threshold to cross, after which you perceive yourself and the world in a totally different light. The event of awakening changes your perspective forever, and along with that, the entire quality of your life.

But once this radical inner shift has occurred, the quality of awakening can still grow richer. It can flower into further fullness as the awakened one not only abides as formless consciousness, but also progressively integrates the aspect of reality that is form into his realiza-

173

tion. The human side especially, with all its idiosyncrasies and shadow residue, often requires further evolutionary polishing, in order to better attune it to the new reality of awakened awareness.

So, awakening does not immediately and automatically saturate all aspects of the body-mind with non-dual presence, thereby bringing one's development to its final conclusion. Rather, it heralds the beginning of a further maturation process. Awakening is an endless unfolding.

The realization of formless emptiness will always be the base, as well as the primal requirement for an authentic non-dual realization. But it is the form-aspect of reality that is responsible for the fact that awakening matures further, as the awakened one moves through many further post-awakening phases.

Hans: *You just explained how the life stories of many spiritual teachers attest to the phenomenon that shadows are not automatically wiped away by awakening. Yet earlier on you also explained at length how shadow qualities can be transformed by bringing presence to them. If awakened awareness is the quintessential form of presence, then surely awakening must have some advantage to offer in cleaning up shadows?*

Ameen: The way I see it is that awakening *could* offer such an advantage, but that it doesn't necessarily do so... Remember that, no matter how deep your awakening might be, shadows cannot be seen directly, by simply looking within. They are your blind spots. Their home base is your unconscious zone, and getting them back into view requires focused self-inquiry. Even with awakening there is no way around that. So awakened awareness alone is not sufficient for transforming shadows. You also need a willingness to keep scrutinizing your emotional world with self-skeptical humility. But once this willingness is present, awakened awareness can support your shadow work in ways that the un-awakened mind cannot.

One of the first things that stood out for me was that, against the background of the silent equanimity of awakened awareness, you are able to notice emotional perturbations all the more clearly. From the place of rest, prior to the mind, you can quite effortlessly spot even the most subtle movements of your mind. Awakened awareness is alert and open. It is always now. And because it knows no time, it exposes even the tiniest agitations immediately—*as* they arise. So even though, in and of itself, awakening does not make it easier to see your *actual shadows*, it does allow you to spot your *shadow reactivity* with immediacy and much greater clarity. This alone is already a remarkable gain. But if you then also make the effort to actually inquire into your shadow reactivity, the beneficial impact of awakened awareness can reach further as well.

Once you have a good grasp of what your shadow exactly is, awakened awareness also makes it easier to address the issue, transform it, and eventually release it—because you are no longer in the grip of the ego.

Before awakening, the ego is still the basic structure around which all your shadow voices and characterological wounds cluster; it is the core to which they are all directly connected. As long as this primary structure is still intact, the secondary shadow voices tend to stay intact as well. They are part of the ego complex that wants to uphold itself, defend itself, or deny its own shadows. All these egoic forces complicate real progress in shadow work.

But the moment you wake up, you land in a different world. Your egoic structure appears to be fluid, as the contracted density has disappeared from it. Your ego and its shadows are no longer experienced as fundamental to who you are. You have recognized yourself to be pure presence; formless, empty and unqualified. And from that perspective, there are no unwanted qualities to repress, reject, or deny anymore; no unwished-for emotions to withdraw or dissociate from. All your defense strategies have lost their ground in the radical openness of spirit, where all is one, and nothing remains to defend yourself against. Their reason for being has disappeared. So you no longer feel the need to tinker

175

with the less flattering realities of your darker side. Nothing needs to be swept under the rug any longer. The infinite spaciousness of awakened awareness provides plenty of room for the whole 'you'. Its all-inclusive openness allows you to embrace your flaws as well, with radical self-acceptance. All these qualities that come along with awakened awareness make it easier to take an honest, no-nonsense look at your own stuff, and expose it for what it really is.

So awakened awareness, in my view, *can* indeed make shadow work more effective, and lighter to go through. But whether it actually *does* so or not depends first and foremost on your willingness to look your shadows squarely in the eye, and acknowledge them. In the end, it all comes down to this: Are you courageous and truthful enough to recognize the areas in yourself where there is still dissonance in your expression—where your words or deeds are not yet as aligned with the inherent purity of consciousness as they could be? So the actual success of your shadow work will always lean more upon the depth of your sincerity, than upon the depth of your awakening.

Hans: *I have heard several spiritual teachers acknowledge that they still have shadows, but that they were also very reluctant to engage in shadow work in a psycho-therapeutic setting, because they felt that a therapist could not understand the nature of their awakened state, and the way it affects the capacity to handle shadows. Do you think this is a legitimate concern?*

Ameen: Let's put it this way: when you call on someone to fix the bumper of your car, you don't need that person to know everything about the engine of the car as well. It is always useful to seek out the guidance of people with expertise in certain areas of human functioning and learn from them. They don't need to know every single thing about you, in order to be able to help you. Working together with experts can only support you in your quest to come to a more comprehensive understanding of who you really are, and how you function. These people help you connect you to your shadows; they help you form an understanding about how your shadows were created, and how they manifest in your life. Such are the outlines of their job description. If they do that well, that's sufficient. They do not necessarily need to be aware of the formless reality beyond the shadows. But after they have done their job, it's up to you to create the synthesis, and apply their contribution to the totality of who you are. In the end, nobody but you can put all the pieces of your puzzle together—and thus, the final responsibility for the totality of your process rests with you.

So in my view, even if you are awakened, it can still be useful to consult with a psychiatrist or a therapist... At least, this is how I approach this matter in my own life. Even after awakening, I still visited my therapist on a regular basis. She was aware of my state, but treated me like she treated everybody else. From the beginning of our work together, her stand has always been that my awakened state could be used as an escape—and she was right. She urged me to focus on my shadows, rather than being distracted by the benefits of my state—and so whenever we met, we always went straight to my issues.

But in a way, I also understand the concern you described, and that many awakened teachers seem to have. I have to admit that I also sometimes felt that my therapist didn't recognize the influence of awakened awareness sufficiently. It is true that waking up changes the texture of your personality complex. After awakening, it is no longer thick with ego, and its fluidity has a positive effect on your capacity to handle shadows—as we discussed earlier. So it would be great if there were more therapists who could understand the complexities of how presence impacts shadow work. But as long as we haven't reached that point, it is probably more important to remember that shadow is still shadow—whether before or after awakening.

Hans: *So how does this idea of the co-existence of shadow and awakening translate into the student-teacher relationship? Some teachers have a rather harsh teaching style. They do not, like others, offer you sweet advice, a gentle smile, or a pat on the back. They are confrontational—in your face all the time. Some even use shock tactics, or deliberately set up crises for their students—just to wake them up, rattle them out of their egoic complacency, or help them break through their boundaries. But these tough teaching methods don't always seem to end well. Some students claim to have been damaged by them and they interpret the harshness as the result of residual shadow material in the teacher.*

But I have heard spiritual teachers push back against this expla-nation, insisting that their interventions actually come from a higher level of wisdom and development—and that their ways cannot yet be accurately understood by the student, because nobody can adequately assess that which is still over their head. So they main-tain that, even if their intervention might, at first glance, look like problematic shadow behavior, in reality, it is actually an expression of skillful means in service of the student's further evolution—and simply dismissing it as shadow behavior, just because it upsets your ego, is an all too easy way to let yourself off the hook.

How do you relate to this argument?

Ameen: Well, there is surely some truth to it, and we shouldn't be too quick to judge these situations. A teacher-student relationship can be very rich, very intense, and very complex, so it can be hard to assess what is really going on.

It *is* true that when you wake up, you have undergone a radical shift in perspective, in a way that is not unlike waking up in the morning and remembering your dream from the night before. However real your dream might have felt to you at the time, now that you have woken up, you know that it was just a dream. With awakening, a shift of sim-ilar proportions occurs. Right now, your day-to-day waking state, and everything in it, feels real, solid and concrete to you. But when you wake up as the true self, your entire 'ordinary' waking state is perceived to be a dream, as your base of identification has now shifted to consciousness itself. From that state you truly *can* see where others are still sleepwalking, and you *can* make corrective suggestions in order to help them wake up.

But there are caveats to be made here as well. A big one is exactly what we have been talking about the whole time: that *nobody*, however deeply awakened, is entirely shadow free. Even if your overall consciousness has woken up from the dream, your shadows are still very much part of the dream—and moments of shadow reactivity are moments of dozing off a little again. This means that, despite all the awakening wisdom a genuine teacher can offer, teaching expressions that are less than awakened will always be part of the teacher-student relationship.

So some of the shock tactics used by some teachers, indeed, originate from an awakened perspective and good intention, and can help the student grow. Others, however, come from shadow residue and don't necessarily do much good. And in most cases, it is probably an intricate mixture of both wisdom and shadow, which makes it even harder to assess the situation.

One of the best ways to differentiate between shadow and wisdom is still your own plain old bullshit detector. If you notice some recurrent pattern in the teacher's ways, some proclivity that still feels somewhat narrow, contracted or emotionally charged—and it's not your own projection—that's probably not the wisdom of the great awakening coming through. If you are courageous enough to scrutinize not only the teacher's, but your own motives as well, you will surely find out what is real. In your heart, you already know the truth anyway. Your own sincerity will always point you straight to it.

I should probably add that I am not such a teacher. It is just not in my nature to take up heroic struggles with my students' karma. I see myself

179

more like a partner and a guide who can give advice when asked, and who can help you see your own egoic tendencies with greater clarity. But in the end, the responsibility for your growth process is your own. Too much power has been handed over to teachers by students over millennia of spiritual practice. Students have all too often projected their own often somewhat naïve and immature images of superhuman greatness or perfection upon the teacher. Sometimes the teacher clings to his authority by mirroring these projections and reflecting them back to his audience—and sometimes not. I love to relate to my students in a spirit of mutuality, and I make it a point to be open and transparent about my own humanity and vulnerabilities.

Guiding people through their awakening process is a fine art, and the skillful means to do so don't just land in your lap the moment you wake up. You need to cultivate them with patience and care. Over the years, I went through a learning curve about how to approach people and relate to them. When I began to teach, my partner used to tell me that I was too direct with people about their shadows. She noticed how it tended to shut them off. That was a mistake. It was too blunt. Many people had never meditated before and were not yet sufficiently connected to their witnessing awareness to be confronted with their shadows the way I did. Now, I am somewhat more skillful in seeing who is in front of me and addressing them appropriately. And I am aware that there will always be more for me to learn.

If you choose to work with a spiritual teacher, my suggestion would be to find out which type of teaching style works best for you. If you have a particular path in mind, ask yourself whether you feel truly drawn to its teachings, and notice whether you feel a heart connection with the teacher. If so, try out this path for some time—and then assess your progress. If you find yourself more alive, more sane, more free and more aware, then you may very well have found your path... In the end, always keep in mind that the main role of a spiritual teacher is to facilitate your awakening. This is the yardstick. And even though awakening is a mystery you can find only in the silence of your own heart, still a spiritual teacher can be an invaluable ally in your quest. Just being in relationship with him or her can wake up the heart's mystery in you—for he or she is already awake to it.

5

Depths of Awakening

Hans: *Your awakening occurred right in the middle of a time when a big wave of so called Neo-Advaita teachings was flooding the spiritual scene. These teachings emphasized, above all else, the importance of recognizing one's true nature as absolute consciousness. But as your own post-awakening process unfolded, you came to understand that such a recognition was more like a first step. So you began to distinguish between recognizing awakened awareness and truly being it. Can you clarify this further?*

Ameen: Sure. I began to see this distinction by observing how the quality of my awakening deepened over the years. So probably the best way to give you a real feeling of the difference between them is to talk about the actual changes I observed in myself during my post-awakening years.

Right after awakening, I was mostly in a state of nothingness beyond everything. At times, I was so absorbed in the self-radiant reality of consciousness that nothing else seemed to even be real. Even my own body seemed no more substantial than the air. I had recognized my true nature as absolute consciousness and was utterly detached from everything relative. During those days I was simply present—nothing more. Just looking... like an owl. *(laughs)*

This was right around the time that my father died. I can still remember how I experienced his burial from that state—and it will not sound warmhearted... His body was just something that they put into the ground. I didn't really feel that I had lost a father, or even that I had had a father. Nothing was taken away from me. The notion of a 'father' was just a concept in the mind. The way in which I experienced his funeral made the impersonal nature of my state very apparent.

It was obvious to me that formless consciousness was the primary reality, whereas the entire world of form appeared to be an illusion, somewhere in the periphery of my awareness. The sense of oneness, the beauty, and the inherent clarity of consciousness were so compellingly attractive that I wanted to be absorbed in it all the time. I didn't want to get entangled in any of the imperfections that always come along with engagement in this world. Everything manifest felt so insignificant and fleeting in comparison with the profundity of formless consciousness. During that early post-awakening period, I clearly privileged formless-ness over form.

As you said, back then, 'Neo-Advaita' was powerfully present in pop-ular spiritual culture—so much so, that it radiated an aura of being the reference for those who, like myself, did not have a broader spiritual background. So, hoping to find greater clarity about the nature of my awakening, I attended several 'Neo-Advaita' satsangs. I soon found that I could easily relate to the core teachings of non-duality in this format, as again and again, they articulated that the world of form is illusory, and that consciousness alone is real. These declarations affirmed my own understanding at the time.

But as my post-awakening process unfolded, I began to grow increasingly uncomfortable with the extreme emphasis in those circles on this specific teaching tenet—probably because I began to feel that I overvalued it myself. I felt particularly uneasy with what I perceived to be a strange cynicism towards all things relative: our humanness, emotional sensitivities, the body-mind, our relatedness to others, and so on. Treating everything as an illusion tends to create an atmosphere of trivialization, even dismissal—not one in which life is deeply entered into, and wholeheartedly embraced.

Sometimes, these 'Neo-Advaita' satsangs were filled with dismissive laughter about the joke of the illusory nature of the ego and the world. Only the absolute reality was ultimately valued. Some teachers even made a mockery of their own physical body and its health. I remember one of them smoking during satsang, laughing it away with the often-heard Neo-Advaita slogan: 'I am not the doer', and then glibly adding: 'Smoking happens.' Many Neo-Advaita proponents seemed to hold the view that whatever the current state of the body-mind is, even if it is unhealthy or seriously put at risk, everything is essentially fine, as long as you recognize your true nature as the absolute. This strange cynicism towards the form aspect of existence was even considered to be a sign of spiritual maturity—solid proof that you had understood the teaching.

To me, this attitude didn't feel entirely authentic. Even if form appears to be illusory, it still *is* arising. Just like formlessness, form carries a legitimacy of its own—an integrity that needs to be honored. My intuition told me that the tendency to trivialize form was probably more rooted in shadow issues and other forms of avoidance than in genuine clarity and radical understanding.

So being exposed to these teachings helped me clarify my own bias towards formlessness at the time. It was as if they were holding up a mirror to me—a mirror in which I began to see how my own absorption in the self-radiant beauty of the empty state was turning into an escape strategy to avoid the challenges of daily life. I also began to grasp that my immersion in emptiness was an excellent alibi to not have to face my shadows, since they didn't really bother me there.

With these insights, it began to dawn on me that my preference for abiding in the empty state perpetuated a sense of distance from life. This was not in sync with my truest heart's desire, which had always steered me towards the deepest possible intimacy with life. Yes, I did perceive life to be an illusion in one sense, but I could also begin to feel a natural urge to reconnect to the illusion—to re-embrace life.

As a response to this urge, several post-awakening developments were set in motion—all of which conspired to fulfill my heart impulse to become deeply intimate with life.

The crystallization of the mind cleaned out residual shadow material that still caused moments of disconnection from life. The emergence of my soul-nature awakened a sense of purpose in life, which compelled me to engage with it more fully. A further shift in my state of consciousness, in which form and formlessness revealed themselves to be one seamless whole, further uprooted my sense of being separate from life.

Whatever else I could say about these distinct processes, the bottom line was that they were all carried by one single underlying direction: a movement into life.

After six to seven years, this movement felt as if it had reached a certain completion. It had transformed the entire quality of my realization. Awakening, to me, was no longer only the mere recognition that my true nature was pure consciousness. It had now also permeated me more fully, and it felt more deeply embodied.

The difference between the two qualities of awakening is like night and day. Looking back on it all, it is clear to me that the recognition of our true self as consciousness is just the first step. Still, it is a deeply significant realization. It means that our perceptual faculty has touched in with pure consciousness. As a result, you *know* with incontrovertible clarity that you are, at heart, consciousness itself. This knowing has become your tacit recognition.

But *recognizing* your true nature doesn't guarantee that you can also really *live* it. Living your true nature requires a further maturation process that does not just include your perceptual faculty alone. It also includes all the other dimensions of your being. They too need to be further purified, refined, and reorganized around your true nature as consciousness. As this process deepens, qualities reflective of pure consciousness, like silence, clarity, freedom, and a sense of wellbeing, will begin to radiate through you more readily—and you become a fuller translation of consciousness into life; a more generous expression of the awakened state, if you will.

This, at least, is how I observed my own post-awakening process unfold. What I was so grateful for was that the more embodied my awakening became, the more fully it allowed me to inhabit life—the very thing I had always so deeply longed for.

In hindsight, it is now clear to me that, during those early post-awakening years, the quality of my realization as the absolute was still lacking something. It carried a bit of a sterile quality—a luminous yet cool beauty—devoid of the human warmth of an all-embracing heart. Only with the unequivocal inclusion of the world of form, with all of its imperfections, humanness, and vulnerabilities, the cool beauty of the absolute thawed, and transformed into a quality of warm embrace. By preferring to abide as the absolute, I had unknowingly been shielding myself from the vulnerabilities of the world of form, and from my own human fragility as well—and that had kept my heart closed.

As I further matured, my love of form grew, and it awakened a sense of intimate familiarity with life. Even the dark side of life began to feel familiar to me. I no longer wanted to detach myself from the suffering, the injustice, the violence; or avoid it at all costs—because it too began to feel as if it was somehow endowed with an inherent perfection. A couple arguing, a baby screaming, a husband murdering his entire family for God knows what reason... all of it, however horrific, now appeared as but the poem of existence. My heart was blown wide open—available to include it all. The quality of my awakening had morphed into a sense of wholeness that was deeply pervasive.

I had finally come to understand that true freedom is not the great escape into emptiness that I had tended to make of it during my early post-awakening years. And I had seen that, even if we have realized the

187

great state of *freedom from life*, as long as any of our form-aspects—body, mind, or soul—have not yet been fully inhabited and brought into a condition of basic sanity, our *freedom in life* is bound to remain partial.

6

Our Soul-Nature

Hans: *Following the call of your soul-nature seems to have played a vital role in your interior growth process—both before awakening and afterwards. It supported you in upholding your authenticity all the way through. Still you sometimes seem reluctant, or cautious, to talk about the soul explicitly. Why is that?*

Ameen: I always treat the soul as a very delicate matter. There are several reasons for that. The most obvious one is that our soul-nature is not something that is clearly discernable, especially if we are still in the earlier phases of the awakening process. It is not something that you can simply identify, and start working with, the way you can with the mechanisms of your mind. Your soul-nature is more subtle, refined, intuitive, and deeply personal. You can envision it as the most intimate, personal dimension of your own being—a presence that is specifically 'you', and that has always been there, for as long as you can remember. It is that which inspires you to express yourself in your own unique way.

Because it is so ephemeral, it is hard to speak about this in non-poetic terms... It is the source of your intuition; your sincerity. It is present in that quiet, tender place you touch in with a few minutes before you fall asleep. It is that which is touched when the moody beauty of a sunset takes your breath away; or when your heart skips a beat when you are swept up for a moment in the euphonious chords of a Bach fugue.

If you listen deeply, with a quiet mind, you may pick up on the many subtle ways in which this innermost sacred part of you informs you. You may have intuitions about who you truly are on the deepest personal level. You may have a distinct sense about why you are here; about your destiny. You may have a knowing about what it is exactly that wants to self-express through you; or about what your role in life is to be. Deep inside you already know all these things. You can sense them, because they are the voices of your own unfulfilled potentials. So, having these glimpses of your soul-nature can be most catalytic for your further growth. They can show you the road ahead.

The pitfall is that, sometimes, when people have some intuition of who they truly are, and what they are here to do, the mind grabs on to it and concretizes it prematurely—while it is in reality still nothing but an amorphous potential. Then, they become so taken in by this concrete picture of what they imagine they are meant to be that, rather than fully showing up in the present, they suddenly find themselves living in some projected future. Meanwhile, the aliveness of the present moment continues to elude them.

That is why, when it comes to these types of intuitions of your soul-nature, it is always helpful to remember your actual condition of unknowingness. Nobody knows for sure where life will take them. The future you dreamed up for yourself, even if it is based on some authentic intuition, may eventually turn out to be nothing but a vain fantasy. Sometimes your life conditions simply won't allow you to manifest your greater potentials the way you had envisioned them. Perhaps there is a war; perhaps you are handicapped or penniless. Therefore it is good to remember that the concrete form of your expression is not the main point. Even under unfavorable circumstances, you can still find ways to express yourself that are perfectly in sync with your soul-nature—even if they are not entirely compatible with your expectations or future ideals.

If your unique quality of self-expression is singing, for example, you don't necessarily have to become a professional singer, performing for appreciative audiences in the Met. From the perspective of your soul-nature, it doesn't matter whether you are singing in the bathtub or in the opera. *How* it is done is not as important as *that* it is done. So however compelling your intuitions might feel to you, don't turn them into some rigid goal without which you will never feel complete. If you start to believe that you can only be happy or fulfilled if you manage to make your vision happen, then your attachment to your vision will turn into a cause of suffering.

Yet sometimes, the pitfall turns out to be the exact opposite response... Rather than inflating your intuitions into premature concretizations, you may also simply not want to hear what your soul wants you to know.

Perhaps you live with the uneasy sense that some aspect of your life, in which you are deeply invested, is not right for you. You simply *know* it is not the path to your greater fulfillment. Perhaps you are in a relationship you shouldn't be in, but you don't want to disrupt your emotional equanimity by doing what you know deep inside is right for you. Perhaps you are spending your days in a monotonous job that stifles your aliveness. Still, you dare not take that leap into the unknown and quit this job, because it offers you financial security. Perhaps you strongly feel you have a mission in life, but are afraid to dive into it completely, because you know it would require life changes that scare you.

Whatever the case may be, it is not uncommon that the aspirations of your soul thrust you into a different direction than the one your egoic identity encourages you to follow—and you might not see how you can answer your soul's call without disrupting the smooth flow of your life.

Still... no matter how long you keep resisting, in the end, your deeper knowing *cannot* be denied. The force of your own authenticity will continue to call you out, and sooner or later you will need to surrender to it—and start living your truth.

So the soul is delicate terrain. Its voice can be so subtle that you only hear it vaguely, or not at all. Hearing it requires a silent mind. Yet when you do pick up on its intuitions, they can feel so true to you that you may either tend to grab on to them and reify them; or you get so afraid of what it would mean to actually follow up on them that you may tend to deny them altogether.

Because the soul is such a tender reality, very susceptible to egoic grasping, I only speak about it upon occasion, and always with some caution. But despite all these caveats, your soul-nature *does* play a valuable role in your life—a role too meaningful to simply ignore. It is the source of your authenticity; your very own voice at the deepest possible level—and I can't think of anything more precious than that. Your authenticity, after all, is what guides you along your path...

Hans: *Right. So how can we align ourselves more fully with that deeper part of ourselves, and include it in our lives in the right way? Can you unpack this a little further?*

Ameen: Sure... Basically, your soul-nature begins to emerge when you are moving into a state of awareness I call 'being'. In being, the grasping activities of the ego begin to relax; and the habitual energy of the mind begins to lose its compulsivity. Your heart softens. Your mind becomes more quiet and clear. And in that silent clarity, your subtle nature—hidden right beneath the constant chatter of the mind—begins to disclose itself. As this happens, the more subtle qualities of your being begin to announce themselves to you.

For some people these qualities will tend to be more phenomenal and remarkable. They may experience spiritual states of bliss, ecstasy, mystical unity; or spiritual phenomena, like visions of subtle light, or subtle energies. Sometimes, inspiring moments of creativity or deeper insights may arise out of nowhere. For others, the qualities they enter into will tend to be more feeling-oriented and less phenomenal. They may experience a sense of profound fulfillment, wellbeing, genuine love, great joy, freedom, serenity, intimacy... The deepening into being can express itself in you in many different ways.

The bottom line is that, in being, an entire inner world of a more subtle nature begins to come alive in you—and this overall deepening is the context in which your soul-nature begins to become more pronounced as well.

So the move into being is a welcome unfolding in our awakening process. But even so, we should also remain aware that being is still an intermediate phase—and it needs to be treated as such. It is not yet most radical awakening, in which the ego and the mind are conclusively transcended. In being, you are still identified with your ego and your mind, even though they are no longer running you exclusively. This means that anything you can experience in being may still be infused with the grasping activities of the ego and the mind. This is something to be mindful about, as there are many ways in which the ego can grab on to a true, deep experience and thereby compromise your spiritual progress.

Some people become overly fascinated with the more subtle energies they can access, when they begin to move into being. Subtle phenomena and experiences can be so attractive that you may be tempted to want to hold on to them. As you revel in their magnetism, you may easily forget about radical awakening—prior to any and all experiences. Subtle experiences can feel so overwhelming that their deep impact leaves you convinced that 'this is it!'... But it is not yet it. Being is not an endgame, and more awaits you on the horizon.

So whenever you do experience these subtler qualities, just enjoy them. Remember that, like any other experience in your life, they too will come and go. Their nature is impermanent. They are not the point. They are the by-product of an overall deepening that is taking place— and that broader deepening is really what has the greater value.

Sometimes, the ego latches on to your authentic spiritual deepening by weaving some story around it. You glamorize what is happening to you, and who you are. Whenever that occurs, your new-found depth easily turns into all too colourful forms of esotericism or spiritually romantic ideas that are—again—no longer serving your radical awakening. Before you know it, the story has become more prominent than the actual experience that triggered it. You end up taking on some new egoic identity, rather than transforming the very force of identification itself. You forget that your innermost truth is more sober, simple and silent, and you get side-tracked.

Almost everybody runs into this tendency at some point in their lives. But it is also, for example, a phenomenon we see, at times, in New Age spirituality. Most New Age adherents are truly in touch with this deeper dimension of themselves I call being. Yet some of their colorful, mythic-magic convictions carry the fingerprints of the ego, embellishing authentic experience. Once this blend between real depth and egoic motives has occurred, it is not easy to separate the wheat from the chaff again. What makes it even harder, in this case, to filter out the egoic influences, is that a significant part of the New Age narrative is built around the fulfillment of egoic desires. It tends to be concerned with questions like: How do you attract the things you want from life? How do you make your dreams come true? How do you create your own reality? New Age culture often emphasizes that you can invite positive conditions and experiences into your life merely by holding positive thoughts and intentions in your awareness. Whether you are seeking good health, money, the fulfilment of your ambitions, or a great relationship—all of it *will* be yours, if only you give it your sincere and undivided attention. Yet, a lot of what people end up wanting are things in service of their egoic fulfillment, and this ultimately undermines their spiritual progress and awakening.

Authentic spirituality is not about making life work for you. Its main flavor is one of deep surrender—a total lack of manipulation. It is about realizing that, in the final analysis, the way your life moves is beyond your control. The only gesture, then, that is left for you to make is to humbly sacrifice your ego into that great mystery that is existence. I am not saying that positive intentions don't have a valuable role to play in

194

life. They clearly have the power to gather our attention, bring it into focus, create a fruitful intensity around some issue, and help us orient in our life course.

But like so many things in spiritual life, this too is a paradox. We have to become capable of holding strong intentions, but in the same breath, be ready to let go of our attachment to their actual outcome. The place where both these opposite truths unite is where authentic living is born.

Some New Age advocates seem to downplay the ego-surrendering part of this paradox. They focus mainly on the power of intention and insist upon results—thereby even going so far sometimes as to put the blame of failure on the practitioner alone, by claiming that whenever he doesn't get the intended result, his intention wasn't pure, consistent or powerful enough. They seem to hold the belief that there are no forces in the cosmos more powerful than the 'I'—which is the very thing authentic spirituality attempts to move beyond—and this is where their assumptions begin to sound like narcissism.

These are just some examples of how the true deepening of being—in which the grip of the ego is loosening up—becomes mixed up again with egoic impulses. I could mention many more. But the bottom line is that, in being, the ego is still alive, and tends to reassert itself. This is simply what it always does. So, anything that can be experienced in being—including glimpses of our soul-nature—can still be hijacked by the ego and the mind, because neither have been fully transcended yet. Once this occurs, it can sabotage your further growth.

This is why some spiritual schools refrain from addressing the domain of being and the emergence of our soul-nature within it entirely. They instead choose to affirm only the absolute reality, because doing so cuts right through all the obstacles and confusion. The straightforward clarity of the radically non-dual teachings rigorously exposes all forms of egoic grasping. It cuts right through all the distractions created by subtle phenomena, and serves as a powerful corrective to colorful New Age interpretations.

Still, I have also all too often seen how the rigor of the non-dual view can be exercised in such an extreme way that it turns into a repression of the truth of being and of our soul-nature. This is not a healthy pathway either. It is not a big secret that any form of repression, of any aspect of ourselves, generates a backlash. The soul is an integral part of who we are as human beings, and it needs to be valued as such. We cannot reduce our entire existence to the absolute alone. The soul is the subtle vehicle of our unique manifestation in life. Simply ignoring it, because it is not yet ultimate non-dual truth, and therefore still illusory, is denying an actual part of ourselves. This sabotages the fullness of our expression in life. Our soul-nature needs to be included. It needs to be given the right kind of attention and care, without turning it into another playground for the ego and the mind.

The best way to do so, in my view, is to always treat it in a way that is informed by the radical understanding of the non-dual orientation. If you remain aware that your soul-nature is not ultimate reality, and you remain sincere, sober and truthful about its intuitions, without turning them into more than they are, the ego will stay out of the game.

But the refined nuance, the spiritual maturity and discernment that all this requires, is exactly why I sometimes come across as cautious about bringing the soul into my teaching work too explicitly. Usually, I kind of bring it in through the back door and keep my primary focus on guiding people to the silence of the absolute.

This approach not only eliminates all the confusion, it is also in line with my personal experience. For me, it took the recognition of my absolute nature first, before the real essence of my soul-nature became obvious as well. Before awakening, it was less distinct, exactly because, when I was still in being, even my deepest intuitions were still mixed with mind and ego. But after awakening, when all the mental-egoic grasping and subtle anxiety had dropped away, a clarity set in, and everything changed. The many dimensions of who I was at the relative level, began to clarify themselves in me—and in that process, my soul began to shine through as well.

I can still remember how, sometime after awakening, I began to notice that, even though I recognized myself to be impersonal consciousness, free from any qualities, there was also still a very distinct personal flavor present. I realized I still had certain longings, feelings and yearnings that sprang up from that innermost personal dimension of myself. As I inquired into them, it became clear to me that these yearnings had nothing to do with strengthening my self-image, achieving actual results, or with any kind of searching mechanism whatsoever. Unlike my desires and yearnings before awakening, these yearnings were entirely free from anxiety. They were not ego-bound—and it dawned on me that they were the stirrings of my soul-nature. Before awakening they had been blurred and burdened by the forces of egoic grasping, but with awakening, as these forces released their grip, my soul-nature began to blossom. The more my mind was further cleansed from its residual habitual energies and shadows, the more the soul's free flow became unblocked, and the more its essence began to express itself.

This liberation of our soul-nature can go very far. As the non-dual teachings always emphasize, in the end, even the soul itself is still a part of our relative identity. It is the most subtle version of the 'I'. So just like the ego, the soul too needs to be transcended. As long as we are still identified with the soul, its qualities remain embedded—and locked up—within the forces of egoic grasping, and cannot flourish unrestrained. As such, our soul's expression will remain incomplete. Only when the soul too is transcended in non-dual oneness—liberated most perfectly—can it flower most fully. And when it does, it enriches our awakening, because its unique qualities are now freely available to us, and can be put in service of our most authentic self-expression *as* emptiness, *in* life.

As I see it, the fullest emergence of our soul-nature is ultimately a post-awakening development. Still, the soul can be a rich source of inspiration before awakening as well. Since it is always present with us as our innermost personal essence, it may call us out at any time, and grant us clues about our unfulfilled potentials—before or after awakening.

Just remember that you cannot force it into fruition. It reveals itself of its own accord. It has its own rhythm. It can't be pushed. But by creating the right circumstances, it *can* be invited... So when you are quiet, listen deeply, and wait... It will gently overtake you, and inspire you along your path.

Hans: *So, if I hear you right, you seem to suggest that the full recognition of the soul-nature after awakening actually enriches realization of the absolute, because it is the instrument to further complete our self-expression in life. How can that which is already absolute be further enriched?*

Ameen: There is a famous Zen proverb: 'Before enlightenment chop wood, carry water. After enlightenment chop wood, carry water.' This saying can spark several insights, but it is often used as the litmus test for genuine liberation. It affirms the unassuming nature of enlightenment and instructs us about the enduring value of beginner's mind.

Yet this statement doesn't tell us much about the reality of the soul-nature, nor does it explain how to integrate your soul-nature into your life. It sprouts from the perspective of the absolute. Thus the Zen master, continuing to chop wood and carry water after enlightenment, can thereby easily overlook his own unique expression, as he emphasizes his absolute 'oneness'. When you are liberated, and your actual expression in life is not consistent with your soul-nature and unique creativity, you will evidently still experience 'oneness', but you won't be as vibrant as when you come to live out your true expression. You would be exactly as free, but you wouldn't be as whole. You would probably still be very Zen about it, and simply get the water and chop the wood. But if you feel deeply into the totality of who you are, and be very sincere about what you find, you would notice that there is still a uniquely personal flavor that is not the ego, and that has nothing to do with separateness. This recognition will move you to want to manifest this personal flavor in your life. It is your unique gift to the world.

Full awakening is not just about *recognizing* our true nature. It is about *expressing* our true nature in life as well—and the unique set of qualities of our soul-nature are the means to do so. Expressing these qualities is what shapes the further completion of the awakened one's lifetime.

If you follow that natural post-awakening stream of your being, absolute consciousness will radiate through you in a more powerful way. Your sense of 'oneness' will further intensify, because it will start to infuse the entirety of your body-mind, and from there, flow freely into the world. Just chopping wood would still be beautiful and full, yet the sense of wholeness related to your relative dimension would not be as complete—unless chopping wood is truly what your unique expression is all about... *(laughs)* So in that sense, yes... expressing your soul-nature *does* enrich your realization of the absolute.

Thank you...

I would like to thank, from the depth of my heart, my dear mother Helen for her friendship, love and care. I feel very fortunate to have such a beautiful relationship with her. Thanks to my brother Danny and my sister Naomi for their love and support. A deep gratitude to my wife Aloka and my son Dhyan for sharing life together in love and laughter. I cherish every moment of it!

I keep a dear space in my heart for Yhodit Cohen, who was my therapist for so many years, for her love and dedication.

I would also like to thank my dear friend Zohar Erel for the long years of friendship and support. Deep gratitude to my friend Ori Dromer for helping getting the book endorsed.

Thanks to my publishers, Julian and Catherine of New Sarum Press, for recognizing the beauty of the book and giving it a chance. Thanks for being such a joy to work with and for all the good laughs!

Thanks to my US book agent Keith Martin Smith for being so accessible and caring and for believing in the book.

Thanks to all the teachers and writers who have endorsed the book: Mooji, Patricia San Pedro, Genpo Roshi, Saniel Bonder, John Dupuy, Cindy Lou Golin and Keith Martin Smith.

Many thanks to the co-creator and writer of this book, Hans Plasqui. Without your dedication and love this book could not have happened!

I would like to thank all of my friends from past and present for sharing this beautiful life together in love and laughter.

—*Ameen*

About the Author

HANS PLASQUI WAS RAISED IN A family inspired by the fresh breeze of the cultural renewal of the postmodern revolution in the 1960s and 1970s. At the age of six he was initiated into the Transcendental Meditation technique of Maharishi Mahesh Yogi—which he practiced on and off, like children do. In his mid-teens, however, his passion for exploring human developmental potential, asking the deeper life questions, and practicing spirituality intensified. He met a spiritual master from the lineage of the renowned Indian guru Swami Muktananda and began an extended period of living in the rarified context of a classical guru-disciple relationship.

For over two decades he imbibed the invaluable gifts of this path — such as the direct awakening power of spiritual transmission, the deepening of transpersonal love, and the unlocking of the deeper reaches of meditative awareness. But despite its remarkable capacity to open up a portal to one's higher nature, he also came up against the limitations of this traditional form of Guru Yoga. And so, he began to widen his horizon, studying numerous different spiritual teachings, philosophies and schools, and meeting with many spiritual teachers from diverse traditions, both in India and in the West.

After he had obtained his master's degree in moral philosophy at the University of Ghent, Belgium, he began to build his professional life as a copywriter, a teacher and a writer.

Around 2000 he began an in-depth exploration of Ken Wilber's Integral Theory and became deeply inspired by its unique capacity to bring together knowledge fields from all directions into one comprehensive world philosophy. This eventually led him to study Wilber's Integral Theory at John F. Kennedy University in San Francisco, California.

In 2007 he met Ameen and was struck by his openness in speaking about a central integral understanding: the many ways in which shadow material can still negatively impact our lives, even after awakening—a notion largely alien to most traditional spiritual paths. While crafting *Sincerity Uncompromised,* he used his writing skills and background in Integral Philosophy to describe Ameen's inner journey of awakening, and distill a structured body of teachings from his words.

He now lives in Ghent with his wife Ann, where he spends most of his time writing and building up Integral Edge—a venture dedicated to advancing integrally inspired initiatives.

You can contact Hans at hans@integral-edge.com.

Contact Ameen

Ameen is currently living in Berlin with his wife and son.

For info regarding private sessions, retreats
and online seminars please go to:
www.ameen-teachings.com

CONVERSATIONS ON AWAKENING

Interviews by Iain and Renate McNay

Conversations on Awakening features 24 unique accounts of
Awakening all taken from transcripts of interviews made for
conscious.tv.

Some of the interviewees are renowned spiritual teachers
while others are completely unknown having never spoken
in public or written a book.

These conversations will hopefully encourage you, inspire
you, and maybe even guide you to find out who you really are.

Conversations on Awakening: Part One
features interviews with A.H Almaas,
Jessica Britt, Sheikh Burhanuddin, Linda Clair,
John Butler, Billy Doyle, Georgi Y. Johnson,
Cynthia Bourgeault, Gabor Harsanyi, Tess
Hughes, Philip Jacobs and Igor Kufayev.

Conversations on Awakening: Part Two
features interviews with Susanne Marie,
Debra Wilkinson, Richard Moss, Mukti,
Miek Pot, Reggie Ray, Aloka (David Smith),
Deborah Westmorland, Russel Williams,
Jurgen Ziewe, Martyn Wilson and Jah Wobble.

Published by White Crow Books.
Available from Amazon in ebook and paperback
format and to order from all good bookstores.
Part one: p.282, ISBN: 978-1786770936
Part two: p.286, ISBN: 978-1786770950

www.conscious.tv